Homo Erectus

HOMO ERECTUS

...AND OTHER POPULAR TALES OF TRUE ROMANCE

JOEL YANOFSKY

NUAGE EDITIONS

Cover design by Doowah Design.
Photo of Joel Yanofsky by Julie Bruck.

Acknowledgements
Several of these essays originally appeared in *MTL, Menz, Roads To, and The Montreal Gazette* in different form. Thanks to all my editors, in particular Alastair Sutherland and Bryan Demchinsky

Thanks to my poker buddies and to Wayne, John and Rick. Thanks also to Elaine Shatenstein, Denise Roig, Dawn Rae Downton, the late Al Greenberg, Ray Kisber, Sally Yanofsky and especially my sisters, Marilyn and Renee.

Published with the assistance of The Canada Council and the Quebec Minister of Culture.
Printed and bound in Canada by Veilleux Impression à Demande.

Dépôt légal, Bibliothèque nationale du Québec and the National Library of Canada.

Canadian Cataloguing in Publication Data

Yanofsky, Joel, 1955–
    Homo erectus...and other popular tales of true romance

ISBN 0-921833-48-2

    1. Man-woman relationships. I. Title.

HQ801.Y35 1996 306.7 C96-900812-0

Nuage Editions, P.O. Box 8, Station E
Montréal, Québec, H2T 3A5

for my parents

CONTENTS

Dumped

Here We Go Again

Epilogue

Preface

There are probably going to be a lot of confessions in this book so I may as well begin with one. Last winter when a woman, a publisher, approached me about writing a book about love and sex from a man's point of view, I began to laugh. I don't mean giggle or chuckle either, I mean laugh hysterically.

I was in a public place at the time, a colleague's book launch, drinking wine out of a box, eating one of those tiny cheese cubes—the kind you only see at book launches—and waiting for my date to show up, the same woman who'd dumped me three months earlier. We were continuing to see each other for a variety of reasons, most of which didn't make any sense. But the real reason, the one that made the least sense, was my unwavering conviction that it was only a matter of time before she fell in love with me—again.

I was also calculating the number of times I'd slept with her or anyone else in the previous six months and I kept arriving at the same uninspiring number: zero. Which was when this actual publisher, who, it turns out, wasn't even drunk, started explaining how she was interested in a male perspective on love and sex and being a man in the 1990s. She was, she said, tired of hearing only what women have to say about relationships and what she really wanted to know, particularly as a woman and a publisher, was what a guy has to say on the subject. Maybe a guy like me.

So I started laughing and I couldn't stop. It got so bad I had the feeling everyone was staring at me. Perhaps because everyone was.

I also had the feeling I used to have in the fifth grade when the teacher, Miss Trelor, a young blonde woman in a clinging cardigan who, to my ten-year-old eyes anyway, looked exactly like Jean Arthur in *Mr. Smith Goes to Washington,* disrupted the class, singled me out, and said, "Well, young man, would you mind sharing the joke with the rest of us? I'm sure we'd all like to know what it is you find so amusing."

I had no reply; I played dumb. I also spent most of the fifth grade developing an enormous crush on the teacher who had embarrassed and chastised me in public (another story entirely). I believed it was only a matter of time before she realized that she was falling in love with me as well. I was funny. I was cute. I did my homework on time. I really couldn't foresee any obstacles.

Now, obstacles are all I see. Women are more confusing than ever, not always a bad thing. Confusing, too, is knowing what it means to be a man. What can I say, Miss Trelor? I still don't know what it is I find so amusing. Except I'm still laughing. That's one of the reasons for writing this book: to figure out what the joke is and, better yet, whom it is on. I can't promise any answers, but I have a few theories.

September 1996

GUYHOOD

"Being male is a personality disorder."
—Carol Shields

Consider the Honeybee

Whenever I am confused or discouraged about what women want from me or what I want from them, whenever I feel love is a mystery I'll never be able to fathom and relationships are more trouble than they're worth, I count my blessings. At least, I keep telling myself, you're no honeybee.

Woody Allen once said that he was at two with nature; in my case, you can double that. I have lived my entire life in the suburbs, never very far, as it turns out, from a shopping mall.

As a child, I refused to go to camp; as an adult, the idea of hiking in the woods or sleeping in a tent appalls me. All of which makes me an object of ridicule and scorn to friends who, despite living in the city, are constantly going on about the joys of nature. My reply is always the same: just try telling the plants, animals and insects who inhabit nature how wonderful it is. I'm not here to defend shopping malls, but there is one thing that can be said for them that can't be said for the wilderness: you can usually walk through The Gap without worrying about anyone trying to eat you.

The concept of the candlelight dinner doesn't exist in the wild either; date rape is *de rigueur* and dying for love is not just a romantic metaphor. For the male honeybee, even getting lucky has its pitfalls. It's not just that the bee's sex life is limited—after all, everyone goes through dry spells—it's tragically abrupt. To put it plainly, the male honeybee's genitals have been known to explode at the moment of climax, giving new meaning to the phrase, "no-win situation."

The male praying mantis is faced with a similar Catch-22. While his head is telling him to maintain a safe distance from the aggressive female praying mantis—"She's no good for you," he keeps reminding himself—his abdomen is saying, "Hey, good lookin'." This is a male praying mantis, remember, so we all know which part of the anatomy wins out. The good news is that nature absolves him of any recriminations or second-guessing about his impulsive behavior. The bad news is that nature does this by having the female praying mantis devour her suitor's head during intercourse, a denouement which even guys who don't like cuddling after sex would probably find disconcerting.

The fate of the male Australian redback spider is better but only slightly. His mate at least waits until after copulation to eat him, making the internal and eternal debate about whether or not to stay the night irrelevant.

But nature can be cruel in less obvious ways too. Take the peacock: all he has to do is show off his elaborate plumage to attract a female. Nothing to it, right? Well, leaving aside the fact that the plumage outweighs him and that it makes him an easy target for predators, there's also something fundamentally demeaning about having to preen and parade around like some sort of feathered Fabio just to get laid. It's no coincidence that the moment mating season is over the peacock sheds his plumage. At least until mating season begins again and again he forgets his pride and his common sense and is back making a spectacle of himself. Indeed, the bigger the spectacle the better.

All of this falls under the category of the things we do for love. Okay, you're no buzzing insect, no spineless invertebrate, no dumb bird or frog or chimp or salmon swimming upstream. You are a human being. You have free will. You are the only animal who can choose not to reproduce. None of which explains why you are willing to attend an Atom Egoyan film festival just because a woman you're attracted to thinks that Atom Egoyan is a cinematic genius.

I'm here to say he is no genius. Spend an evening staring at his *oeuvre*—French for he laid another egg—some time and you'll realize just how undeniable and powerful the sex drive is. Like the praying mantis, your head is telling you: "You don't need this. Get the hell out of here. There's the EXIT sign. Why do you think it's lit up, for God's sake?" Meanwhile, your abdomen, so to speak, is telling you to stay put because when you're through with all this pretentious nonsense you can go back to her place and have sex.

If only it were that simple. Unlike most other species, human beings go out for cappuccino after the movies, which is when your date will ask you what you thought of a particularly annoying scene. If you're still thinking with your abdomen, you will stuff a croissant in your mouth and mumble something about how impressed you were with the filmmaker's stark, uncompromising vision. This is also about the time you will realize that when it comes to making an idiot of himself, the peacock has nothing on you.

That's the trouble with human beings: we think we're better than everyone else. "It's tempting to think of love as a progression, from ignorance toward the refined light of reason," Diane Ackerman says in *A Natural History of Love,* "but that would be a mistake." Ackerman's point is an important one and worth remembering. "The history of love is not a ladder we climb rung by rung," she says, "leaving previous rungs below…. The way we love in the twentieth century is as much an accumulation of past sentiments as a response to modern life."

In other words, evolution makes us do it. Anyway, evolution is the only logical reason I can come up with for why I would jog with my girlfriend. If cocaine, as someone once said, is nature's way of telling you you have too much money, then jogging is nature's way of telling you that you have too much time on your hands.

Still, I'm out most mornings now, trying to keep up with a woman who is in infinitely better shape than me, and there's only one thing on my mind: "Why am I doing this?" The simple explanation is that we just might share a shower when we get back to her apartment. The more complicated explanation is that somewhere in my distant past there must have been an ancestor of mine with a bigger skull and a slightly smaller brain but with similarly short legs and similarly insufficient stamina, chasing after a potential mate, thinking, "Just wait till we get back to the cave."

In the meantime, I'm sweating and panting. My Achilles tendon feels like it's about to snap. My back aches. I have a stitch in my side. I have to pee. Dogs are barking at me. Children are staring. That's when something buzzes past my ear and I realize what I probably should have realized a long time ago: the only significant difference between me and that honeybee is that I can't fly.

The Why Chromosome

The history of the human race is the history of dumb decisions, beginning with the first guy with hairy knuckles who figured he'd give this walking-on-two-legs business a try, thus exposing his genitals to assault from enemies, not to mention ridicule from potential mates. Coincidentally, that's also around the same time the fragile male ego became fragile and the loincloth jockstrap was invented.

Ever since then men have earned and deserved a reputation for keeping everything from our groin to our most heartfelt emotions covered up. For a million years or so one of the questions most of us have managed to avoid asking ourselves was what does it mean to be a man? That's not to suggest that any of us really knew the answer—in fact, I'm willing to bet no one did—we just never worried about it.

Now we worry. Boy, do we ever. Any update on the male gender at the end of the twentieth century wouldn't be accurate if it didn't reveal that men these days seem to be suffering from a bad case of testosterone blues—the lingering feeling that there's something we are supposed to be, but no way of knowing what it is. Are we too sensitive or not sensitive enough? Are we hopeless wimps or macho jerks? Are we dinosaurs? Have we outlived our usefulness? Or are we just fools for thinking so?

Personally, I've never figured out why I can't be sensitive one day and thick as a brick the next. My motto has always been, "I'm a guy, so I'm just guessing." And I can say, without fear of contradiction, that I've managed to live up to that motto.

At least until a few years ago when Bill Moyers interviewed the poet Robert Bly for a series of PBS documentaries and ruined it for all of us who were happily clueless. Moyers asked deep, probing questions; Bly wore a funny vest, played the lute and recited some poems. (That's right: things went from bad to verse.) The series was motivation enough for Bly to write *Iron John,* which made it to the top of *The New York Times* Best Seller List and remained there for more than a year. Not surprisingly, a small library of *Iron John* wannabees followed, offering their own variations on the theme of the New Man and what it's going to take to become one.

Suddenly, guys were not only free to run naked in the woods, beat drums and chests, they were being encouraged to do it. If you couldn't make it to the woods on the weekends, you could always join a support group: sharing your stories in suburban living rooms, church basements and community centres. Best of all, men could suddenly complain about the contradictory nature of being men to our heart's content. We were evolving. We didn't have to pretend to be strong and silent any more. We could be obnoxious and whiny.

Understand, I have nothing against whining. In the absence of real answers to real questions, whining seems to me to be as appropriate a response as any other. I also have nothing against the so-called Men's Movement. I wish good luck and lots of it to anyone trying to clear the way for the New Man, I'm just not holding my breath.

Maybe because the whole notion that there could even be such a thing seems, well, overly optimistic to me. A few years ago, I overheard my aunt, who was seventy-five at the time, complaining about how her new ninety-something beau wanted her to set aside her weekends exclusively for him. "He's always around, crowding me," she said. "What does he want from me? Can't he leave me alone for just one Saturday?" At first, the whole conversation seemed quaint, almost adorable, until I realized she could have just as easily been a teenage girl complaining about an overeager teenage boy or any one of a number of women I know, who keep insisting they just want to be my friend. *Now there*, I remember thinking with equal measures of hope and despair, *is something to look forward to: when it comes to matters of the heart nothing ever changes and nothing ever will.*

And even if it does, who's to say that a New Man will be up to the challenge any more than the Old Man was? Anyone who has ever sat through the latest movie version of *Mission Impossible* knows that new doesn't necessarily mean new and improved.

Which reminds me of the story a friend once told me about her eighty-year-old father. It seems he was home one morning listening to the radio and he heard on the news about an airplane that had crashed leaving Cincinnati. This was the same city his son, daughter-in-law and two grandchildren were supposed to be flying through on the first stop of their vacation. They had also been scheduled to leave around the same time as the crash. He didn't know which airline they were on or quite what to do, but he had an uneasy feeling.

He called for information about passenger lists, but he kept being told by airline officials that it was too early for them to divulge any information over the telephone. Officials took his number and promised they would get back to him as soon as possible. That was just before noon. By late afternoon he still hadn't heard anything, except more news reports of how bad the crash was, and how there were few, if any, survivors.

This is a man who is normally upbeat and optimistic, sometimes to a fault. This is a successful, self-confident man. He wasn't used to fearing the worst and, frankly, wasn't any good at it. Except in this situation he didn't have a choice. He'd already decided not to tell his wife anything. He was determined to keep his fears a secret—mainly to protect her, but also to protect himself from what he presumed would be her hysterical reaction. By early evening, he was sneaking outside with the cordless telephone to call for updates every few minutes. There were none.

By the time his wife went to bed at midnight, he'd been keeping his escalating dread to himself for more than twelve hours and had just about given up hope when the news finally came. His family had not been travelling on that airline. When his wife asked who had called so late, he told her everything and collapsed on the bed beside her, an emotional wreck.

By any contemporary standards of manhood, his behavior would be considered unacceptable. After all, he had acted in a typically condescending manner toward the woman in his life. Didn't she have a right to know what was going on?

He had also acted self-destructively. Men die earlier than women, have higher suicide and alcoholism rates. This kind of stoic behavior is one of the reasons why. Hardly a New Man myself, though a little newer than my friend's father, it's certainly not something I would have or could have done. It would never have even occurred to me not to look for solace and support from the woman in my life.

But powerless to do anything else, my friend's father did the only thing he knew how to do: he kept his fears to himself and he kept quiet. It was an act old-fashioned enough to qualify as prehistoric. It was an act that also made me think that maybe there's still something to be said for prehistoric man. Then again, I could be wrong. I'm a guy, remember, so I'm just guessing.

Impractical Jokes

Before anyone ever heard of male bonding, before guys ever felt the overwhelming need to share our pain and joy, we insulted each other. That's how we showed our affection. I can still rely on my best buddies to make jokes about my height or, more precisely, my lack of it. One old friend, in particular, ends all our conversations with, "I'll speak to you…shortly"—the emphasis on "shortly." The first few times he said it deliberately, pausing to make sure I understood that he was making fun of me. Now, he says it matter-of-factly; now, it's a running gag that doesn't need to be acknowledged. Still, I pretend to notice sometimes and, for his sake, I pretend it bothers me.

But it never really has. One of the first things you learn as a young boy is to "take it." Take it like a man. I'm not sure where the line is in a male child's development, but there is a point at which it's okay to cry when someone pushes you or rides your bicycle longer than they are supposed to and there's a point at which it's not.

But "taking it" also means taking a joke, particularly one made at your expense. Little girls probably don't start out any more sensitive than little boys, it's just that little boys realize early on that there are consequences to being too sensitive. One of the consequences of whining or crying in public is that you will become the butt of more and probably crueler jokes. You will also be beaten up on a regular basis.

This may be why men have such an infinitely more refined appreciation of practical jokes than women do. A few years ago, on April Fool's Day, I played a joke on a girlfriend that was so meticulously worked out, so ingenious (without going into too much detail, it involved a fake letterhead, a forged signature and an untraceable fax transmission) that she told me later that she was about to break up with me and would have if I hadn't revealed to her, at virtually the last moment, that I was only kidding. Later, when I repeated the story to some friends, I noticed that she wasn't taking the same pleasure in it as I was. Two years later, I was still telling the story at every opportunity and she just seemed bored. I recognized the look on her face, the one that said, "Not that again."

I've never had to worry about seeing that look on the face of a male friend on whom I have played a prank. He might protest or pretend to be embarrassed, but I know that deep down he enjoys hearing the story retold almost as much as I enjoy retelling it. I know what he's thinking because it's what I would be thinking under the same circumstances. He's thinking: "I love you, man!"

There are probably lots of complex psychological reasons why otherwise evolved men—men who have no problem, for example, cooking dinner or caring for the children—are still uncomfortable expressing their emotions to each other, but I'm not sure the reasons matter. What matters is that we find other, much more elaborate ways to demonstrate our feelings.

I assumed, when I was in my twenties and attending my first series of stag parties, that my friends and I would watch some X-rated videos or visit a strip club. There were even rumors of someone hiring a prostitute for the occasion. None of which happened. Our plans were much more innocent and far more ritualistic. They always involved the element of surprise—specifically kidnapping our intended victim, blindfolding and transporting him to someone's backyard or garage where we would then strip him down to his underwear, pour beer over his head, smash eggs into his chest and generally treat him as if he were a blank canvas and we were abstract expressionists.

We went to a lot of trouble. In fact, the more trouble we went to the more it seemed that we cared. You could tell who your real friends were by the number of eggs they purchased for the occasion. In the case of one bridegroom-to-be, we doused him once, then cleaned him up, drove him downtown, put a dog collar and leash around his neck, and a sandwich board over his shoulders that said, "The end is near." Then we convinced a young woman in a bar who was painting a mural on the wall to take a time-out and paint his face, after which we handcuffed him to a fire hydrant on Ste. Catherine Street, dumped molasses and feathers on him, and stood by and watched as he was nearly arrested. It's a rule of thumb for stag parties—the closer you come to killing a guy, the more you care about him.

For better or worse, I've grown out of stag parties. The last few I attended did consist of desultory and depressing visits to strip clubs. I like looking at naked women as much as the next guy, but I don't like looking at them when being naked is part of their job description. And while the prospect of a nude woman dancing on a table top for my benefit also has some appeal, worrying about what percentage the tip should be tends to spoil the moment.

A few years ago, as an alternative to strip clubs, a few of us organized a poker game for a friend who was about to be married. We smoked cigars, drank Scotch and ate cheese doodles. The cheese doodles notwithstanding, it seemed like a much more civilized way to celebrate an important rite of passage, so much so we've kept up the game and now play every few weeks. We take the game seriously too, all of us reading up on betting and bluffing strategies and analyzing each other's propensities.

But, for me, the memorable moments have always had less to do with how much money I've won or lost and more to do with who we've been able to embarrass and how badly we've been able to embarrass him. For instance, I remember learning on the day of a game that one of our regular players and his wife had agreed to appear on a radio show to discuss their love life in a sort of local version of *The Newlywed Game*. I taped the show and then called another friend. He had taped it too.

"That was a poem he was reciting, wasn't it?" I asked.

"Actually, I think it was a sonnet," my friend said. "A love sonnet."

"Yes, but did you hear him singing 'Sometimes When We Touch' or was I imagining it?"

Then, in unison, both of us said the same thing: "Doesn't he know we're playing tonight?"

Later that evening, about halfway through the game, we cued up the tape and stopped and started it on a particularly graphic part of the interview. Then sporting turned-around baseball caps on our heads, we serenaded our friend with a rap version of his love sonnet. He confessed afterwards that he had remembered the poker game, but he thought he could sneak one by us. "I didn't think you would all be listening to the radio in the afternoon," he said and we gave him a look that was intended to say, "We're always listening."

From the start, we've looked for every opportunity to tease each other—from combing through high school yearbooks for especially geeky pictures we can then glue to the back of a deck of cards to planting dribble glasses. Each of us dreads the day that we will be the target of some brilliant and humiliating prank. Probably the only thing we dread more is not being the target.

Why Men Really Play Softball

It's always early in the spring, when the grass is beginning to grow again, that I think about what's missing from my life. I try to focus on important matters—like spiritual fulfillment or true love or real estate—but my thoughts inevitably turn to softball.

I guess that's why I have always made my version of a New Year's resolution around major league baseball's opening day and why every April, it has been the same one: "This is the year I will join a softball league." A few years ago, I finally kept that promise to myself and signed up to play second base for a slow-pitch league in the Montreal suburb of Côte St. Luc.

It cost $115 to join the league and $40 more for my 100% polyester powder blue uniform. Although it had been more than fifteen years since I put on a fielder's glove or swung a bat—even longer since I wore polyester—the moment I stepped out onto the infield it all came back to me: the thrill of the grass, the camaraderie, the competition…behaving like a jerk.

Like countless other overage, out-of-shape North American males, I wrapped enough bandages around my wrists, knees and ankles to make a Mummy look neglected and found myself doing two things I thought I'd never do again: calling my teammates—nine men I'd just met—"baby," and stating publicly and repeatedly that "the batter's got the willies."

Maybe I shouldn't be admitting this, but I don't know what "the willies" are. The truth: I never knew. But when I was younger it didn't seem to matter. There is only one important difference between playing ball when you are a kid and when you are an adult: as an adult you keep saying to yourself, "Why am I doing this?"

"Why are you?" a girlfriend asked me the first time she saw me in my stretchy powder blue pants with red stripes down the sides. "Explain it to me again."

Which is always my cue to begin a monologue that would test the fortitude of Job or Cal Ripkin. My monologue about how maybe there are some half-baked, best-selling inspirational authors who learn everything they need to know in kindergarten, but not me. I've learned everything I need to know playing ball.

Spitting is optional.

There are two kinds of men: those who will spit whenever the opportunity presents itself and those who won't. You have to ask yourself, which kind are you? This also applies to scratching yourself and to infidelity.

The umpire is always wrong.

However, there's no point in arguing with him because there's nothing you can do about it. This also applies to employers and to women.

Don't think too much.

Especially in crucial situations. Also applies to sex.

Work on your fundamentals.

Sex again.

Take it one game at a time.

At the risk of sounding like a half-baked, best-selling inspirational author, tomorrow is another day, you know. Even if you mess up in one game, there will always be another game in which you can mess up more. This also applies to life.

"So, you see, baseball isn't like life," I concluded as my girlfriend's eyes glazed over, "it is life. Besides, I want to steal a base, snare a line drive, hit one into the gap, stretch a single into a double, I've missed all that."

"Maybe so," she said, "but it would take more than all that to make me wear powder blue polyester."

She had a point. I had assumed that the reason I wanted to play softball again was because I loved the game, pure and simple. But nothing is that simple, not nowadays, not if you are a man and if you are, like me, pushing forty.

This is a critical time, a time when we are forced to redefine what it means to be a man. Today's male—much too sensitive and much too civilized—needs to be reunited with a more forceful side of himself, with what Robert Bly and others in the men's movement like to call the inner "Wild Man." Bly suggests that the best way to do that is for men to gather in the wilderness. But I wonder if we even need to leave the neighborhood. On a suburban softball diamond, I realized that I was getting in touch with what I like to call my inner "Big Jerk."

This is my theory: deep down all men know they are jerks, and spend too much of their time pretending they aren't. Playing softball, the pretense vanishes. For nine innings, anyway, you can argue with umpires, curse your opponents, scratch yourself on a more or less regular basis, and it's not only acceptable, it's expected. Wild Man, Big Jerk—tomato, tamato.

Actually, the bigger the jerk you are, the better. A couple of incidents from my rookie season stand out. The first one occurred at the start of our second game—we'd won our first game—when the captain of the opposing team got into an animated debate with the umpire, which escalated into an argument and ended with the umpire being informed that "his motherfucking head was going to be ripped off and stuffed down his motherfucking throat."

I made the mistake of suggesting to the opposing captain that he might be overreacting and that all he was really succeeding in doing with this temper tantrum of his was holding up the game. He responded by pointing at the umpire and saying, "He started it."

Then he went on to comment on the color of my uniform—"What's that supposed to be? Baby blue?"—and to call into question my own and my teammate's collective manhood. In the meantime, my teammates—all relatively sensitive, civilized males—held a vote and came to the democratic decision to walk off the field, making my main point, that I just wanted to play ball, a moot one. The game was eventually postponed, called on account of death threats.

The second incident occurred during our final game of the season. We were being clobbered as we had been in most of our games. But despite the lopsided score, the players on the other team were continuing to steal bases—a serious breach of baseball etiquette. Meanwhile, I was getting angrier and angrier. From my position at second base, I was ideally situated to stand in the base runner's way. So I did. We bumped and the bump was followed by a familiar string of colorful curses and threats. I remember one of my teammates pointing out to me that I was behaving childishly. Which is when I pointed at my adversary and said, "He started it."

I was probably ten the last time I punched someone. Still, there was a part of me that wanted to knock this guy out cold. Deck him. There was also a part of me that was desperately looking for a way to back down. My heart was thumping, my adrenalin surging. And just like when I was ten I was more worried about the protocol of the fight—who hits whom first? are any girls going to be watching?—than about being hurt. As it turned out, there was no fist fight. And after the adrenalin stopped pumping, I thought about how I had behaved and came to the conclusion that while I hadn't quite distinguished myself as a Neanderthal, I wasn't exactly civilized either.

Robert Bly maintains that reuniting with our inner "Wild Man" is going to be a long, slow process. If that's the case, I'm not discouraged. I know my team and I have the potential to be Big Jerks, big and jerky enough to go all the way next year. We just have to work on our fundamentals and take it one game at a time.

The Cult of Martha

You don't have to convince me. That's what I said to myself when I read that *Time* magazine had chosen Martha Stewart as one of the twenty-five most influential people in America. In case you've been living in a cave—and a badly decorated one at that—Martha Stewart is a blonde, industrious middle-aged woman who's made a fortune on television and in publishing, selling gracious living. And while some of *Time*'s other choices—like Bill Clinton or Bill Gates—seem like passing fancies, here today, gone tomorrow types, I can attest to the fact that Stewart isn't going anywhere.

Maybe it is a stretch to put her in the same category as presidents and media tycoons. Maybe she isn't really one of the twenty-five most influential people in America, but that's not the point. The point is that she's become one of the most influential people in my life.

Incidentally, this isn't something I'm happy about. But before I explain my reasons for holding a grudge against Martha Stewart, I should probably provide a glimpse into my own domestic life. I am, to put it bluntly, a slob, though, in my own defense, I like to think that I am a well-intentioned slob.

In this respect, I am like a lot of other guys, who are trying, usually without much success, to shake the stereotypical image of the slovenly bachelor. Unfortunately, one of the problems we keep running into is that our best laid plans sometimes end up backfiring. For example, in P.J. O'Rourke's *The Bachelor Home Companion*—"A book about cooking, cleaning, and housekeeping for people who don't know how to do any of these things and aren't about to learn"—O'Rourke offers this clever but ultimately impractical tip: "Bedroom sheets can be kept clean by getting drunk and falling asleep with your clothes on."

See what I mean? This is a man with good intentions and bad instincts. And it's our instincts that always get us into trouble. (This probably isn't a good time to mention my own plan, which would require all clothing to be reversible.) A woman thinks of her home as a reflection of her personality, a showcase of her good taste; a man thinks of it as a multipurpose domed stadium. I've broken lamps, chipped furniture and cracked mirrors playing soccer during the World Cup, football during the Super Bowl, tennis during Wimbledon. I may be the only person in the history of indoor sports who has wall-to-wall carpet burns on his knees from sliding into the living room coffee table.

I know what my problem is: I don't think ahead. Which is why the mess I tend to make around the house is seldom deliberate; in fact, it's practically unconscious. Sure, magazines, candy wrappers, the occasional turkey sandwich, my socks and, it goes without saying, my underwear usually end up under my bed, but this is not entirely my fault. I want to be tidy, really I do. I wish the urge to dust and fold came naturally to me, but it doesn't. Like most men, the message encoded in my DNA says: "Don't worry, I'll do the dishes later."

Of course, it doesn't help that women have ideas about housekeeping that often defy logic. I knew a woman once who would scold you if you actually put garbage in the garbage pail. My sister, with whom I live, has similar ideas about the bathroom towels, which are apparently only in the bathroom to match the wallpaper. I haven't been told this in so many words, but the implication is clear: if I absolutely have to dry my hands I should try shaking them vigorously, at least until the hand driers are installed. Even now in the 1990s, when there is a little more equity in the distribution of household chores, women still understand much better than men the

Sisyphean nature of cooking, cleaning, ironing and all the other countless domestic duties. Women know that doing something once just means you have to do it again. Sometimes, the sheer futility of this must drive them a little crazy.

Which is where Martha Stewart comes in. On her television show and in her bimonthly magazine, she devises household chores and projects that are so intricate and time consuming, so beyond the realm of human possibility, that women can't be blamed for thinking that if they could just follow her example they could escape the drudgery of these tasks by elevating them to the level of poetry. Poets, of course, are also famous for being crazy.

Still, I have to admit that the Martha Stewart phenomenon went completely unnoticed by me until I started becoming aware of some curious changes around the house. Suddenly the dish washing detergent disappeared from its serviceable plastic bottle and appeared instead in a crystal decanter. Otherwise acceptable windows were transformed into mini-greenhouses. Everywhere I looked there was homemade soap, homemade kitchen magnets and homemade bath oils. Paperclips replaced bookmarks—a cookie sheet doubled as a dish rack. The venetian blinds had been replaced by vintage dish towels found at a flea market.

All of these things are, in Martha Stewart parlance, "good things." On television after each of her accomplishments, she stares at the camera and says, "It's a good thing." That's her credo and that she has one at all is what worries me. I don't trust people with credos. You know Joseph Stalin had one and Ayatollah Khomeini and the Reverend Moon.

As for the magazine, *Martha Stewart Living,* not since Mao's *Little Red Book* has a publication seemed so self-righteous and so self-aggrandizing at the same time. She even includes a calendar* at the beginning of each issue so you can keep track of everything she's doing at the precise moment she's doing it—from having her eyes checked to trimming the tree with the First Lady at The White House.

In addition to subscribing to *Martha Stewart Living,* my sister is demonstrating other classic signs of cult behavior: blind obedience, unthinking devotion and a desire to convert me. At the same time, I'm trying to do all I can to deprogram her. Now when I leave my clothes on the floor or dry my hands on the bathroom towels, I do it deliberately. My only worry is that it may be too late.

The other day my sister began talking about preparing a special Easter dinner which called for her to roast a fresh ham "for five hours and serve it garnished with organically grown grass that had been cut early in the morning with the dew still on it."

"Dew?" I asked.

"Yes," she said, setting her alarm clock for dawn.

"Easter dinner? Ham?"

She nodded.

"But it's September," I said, "and we're Jewish!"

"It doesn't matter," my sister said, "It's a good thing." And, you know something, it's becoming harder and harder to argue with logic like that.

* Martha Stewart's calendar, which appears in every issue of her magazine, can be intimidating, particularly to men. But to demonstrate that all our lives are worthwhile in their own unique way, I've compared some highlights from her busy schedule last summer to my own:

Martha Stewart's Calendar	My Calendar
July 2 Sow pansies in flats for setting out in garden in fall	Forgot to mow the lawn
July 12 Go antiquing in Maine	Look under the bed for socks
July 16 Harvest sweet peas	Take a pee
July 30 Weed and water, water, water	Shower (optional)
August 14 Spray roses for mildew and black spot	Huh?
August 17 Paella party on beach	Make a sandwich and watch beach volleyball on TV
August 30 Divide peonies	Reunite peonies

SEX VS. ROMANCE

"Sex relieves tension, love causes it."
—Woody Allen

Postmodern Romance

I am suggestible. It's not just that I believe everything I read, I believe everything I read while I'm waiting in line at the supermarket. So don't try telling me there are no UFO's and that Michael Jackson isn't the result of a bizarre reproductive experiment pairing a human father with an alien mother. There are and he is. I know because I read it somewhere.

But it's Hollywood, in particular, that has my number. If the whole point of the movies is to mesmerize the audience and convince them that what they are watching up on the screen is actually happening—at least for the brief time they are watching it—then consider me mesmerized. Sometimes I'll even leave the movie theatre thinking Richard Gere can act. I am a sucker, in other words, and I'm reborn every ninety minutes or so.

Which is why I can sympathize with parents and politicians who are worried about all the violence portrayed in movies and on television and who are genuinely concerned about the detrimental effect it may have on young, impressionable viewers. Still, if you ask me, all these concerned people are wasting their time and barking up the wrong tree. We don't need less violence in the movies, we need more.

Let the explosions and shootouts, the car chases, karate kicks and decapitations continue. Let Sylvester Stallone go on throwing punches and Arnold Schwarzenegger keep on terminating. Give Quentin Tarantino an unlimited budget and let the fake blood flow. My reasoning is simple: the more violence there is on the screen the less room there will be for the truly hazardous stuff...all those movies that keep telling us that we are destined to live happily ever after.

As a kid, I used to spend hours pretending I was a swashbuckling Burt Lancaster in *The Crimson Pirate* or a fast-drawing Alan Ladd in *Shane* and it didn't do me any harm. I grew up watching westerns, war movies and sci-fi thrillers, none of which has—so far anyway—transformed me into a bloodthirsty psychopath.

I've also spent most of my adult life reading and studying twentieth century literature, the theme of which is obvious to anyone with a Hi-Liter: nothing lasts forever, especially love. What else was Marcel Proust on about when he said that "in love we cannot choose but badly"? What was the point of the last pages of James Joyce's "The Dead" if not to reveal to the story's silly, sentimental protagonist that his beloved wife was thinking about someone else the whole time he thought she was thinking about him?

But despite all this, it's the mushy stuff in those old movies—the boy-meets-girl, boy-loses-girl, boy-gets-girl theme in all its variations—that still gets me every time. Bogie and Bacall. Hepburn and Tracy. Cary Grant and Rosalind Russell. Jimmy Stewart and Jean Arthur. Even Rock Hudson and Doris Day have me convinced.

The cumulative effect on me is obvious to anyone who knows me: I'm a romantic fool. But at least I'm not alone. Just ask yourself which are there more of in the world: serial killers or people who think they are going to live happily ever after and you have your answer. A fact I find a lot scarier than any Stephen King plot.

This is my conspiracy theory: Hollywood planned it this way all along, even going so far as to subvert the nation's literature. It's no coincidence, for example, that the first movie version of Tennesee's Williams melancholy play *The Glass Menagerie* had a happy ending tacked on, in which the narrator's lonely, crippled sister Laura has a successful operation to repair her clubfoot, finds a husband and has a family. The same kind of thing was true of the 1949 version of F. Scott Fitzgerald's *The Great Gatsby*. In this case, Hollywood couldn't bring the title character back to life so they gave the narrator, Nick Carraway, a loving wife, the same woman who, in the novel, comes to represent everything Nick Carraway despises. A blind faith in monogamy and unambivalent love remains Hollywood's most premeditated and enduring contribution to the North American psyche.

Last summer, on the occasion of his ninetieth birthday, Billy Wilder, who directed and co-wrote classics like *Sunset Boulevard* and *Some Like It Hot*, admitted in an interview that he doesn't know what to tell people when they ask him what *The Apartment*—one of his most popular movies—was about. "I say I don't know what the theme is. I just thought here is comedy, here is tragedy. That is the way life is. I just tried to do it true to life," he explained.

There's never been any doubt in my mind that Billy Wilder is a genius and, by all accounts, a charming man. But who does he think he's kidding? He knew exactly what he was doing when he made *The Apartment* and it's about time unsuspecting viewers knew too.

The Apartment, which was released in 1960 and won the best picture Oscar for that year, tells the story of a naive young bachelor—played by Jack Lemmon with a kind of Everyman mix of spunk and put-uponness—trying to succeed in the dog-eat-dog world of business and also find happiness in a big, impersonal city. Success, at least, turns out to be no trouble at all.

Wilder's hero is rapidly climbing the corporate ladder in a giant insurance company by loaning his apartment to his superiors who are, in turn, using it as a hideaway for their numerous infidelities. Lemmon plays along and keeps his mouth shut. Glowing recommendations and promotions follow. Until the president of the company, Fred MacMurray, playing against type as the bad guy, calls Lemmon in to confront him. He knows about Lemmon's distasteful scheme to succeed in business without really working and he is not amused.

MacMurray gives his employee a long, self-righteous talking-to about the importance of propriety and about how it only takes a few rotten apples to spoil the whole barrel. Then he asks Lemmon for the key to the apartment. He has a mistress, too, and needs a convenient, discreet place to meet her. Lemmon can't believe his luck. He hands over the key, his future in the company assured, and mutters, "What's one more rotten apple, percentagewise?"

The conflict in Wilder's plot arises when the woman MacMurray is bringing to the apartment is the same woman—played by Shirley Maclaine—that Lemmon is falling in love with. The audience knows about this long before Lemmon does and we are devastated, in advance, on his behalf.

Meanwhile, Maclaine, who is ashamed of herself and the way she has allowed herself to be used, takes an overdose of sleeping pills. Lemmon finds her in his apartment and saves her life. Two lonely people have discovered each other and the story is set in motion, on the way to its inevitable happy Hollywood ending. But that's the thing about *The Apartment*—it shouldn't have a happy ending or at least we shouldn't be so eager to accept one.

After all, Wilder is no hack and the whole premise of his clever, bitter story is that infidelity is commonplace in the modern world and so is hypocrisy. Everyone has their eye on the main chance and the bottom line and everyone uses everyone else. Maclaine is lovely in this movie and she's also smarter than any of the other characters. She knows, as she tells Lemmon, that the world is made up of two kinds of people: "Those who take and those who get took." She also has the movie's most uncompromising and heartbreaking lines. "Why do people have to love people anyway?" she asks Lemmon. Later she asks him again, "Why can't I ever fall in love with someone nice like you?" To which Lemmon, who is already crazy about her but realizes there is no point in saying so, responds, "That's just the way it crumbles, cookiewise."

The movie should end there, but it doesn't. Cynical, witty and sad, *The Apartment* gives us the truth about relationships and then takes it all back. In the final scene, true love triumphs, against all the odds, as Shirley Maclaine and Jack Lemmon play gin rummy and live happily ever after.

I've watched this movie at various stages in my romantic life—when I was alone, when I was in love, when I was just out of love—and each time I've always had the same two conflicting reactions. First, it makes me cry like no other movie does, then it makes me furious at myself for crying.

We live in a postmodern age. Self-consciousness is our most comfortable posture. Irony is everywhere, like the air we breathe. In this respect, *The Apartment,* even if it is pushing forty, is a kind of postmodern romance. At least for me it is. Each time I watch it I can't help feeling that Billy Wilder is winking at me. "Admit it," he is saying, "this is what you really wanted all along. Don't blame me, don't blame Hollywood. You're the suggestible one."

He's right. I grew out of wanting to be a pirate and a cowboy, but when the music swells at the end of the movie and Shirley Maclaine walks out on Fred MacMurray so that she can return to the person the audience knows she was meant to be with all along, I'm an impressionable kid again. That's what so insidious and so irresistible about Billy Wilder's story. Despite all evidence to the contrary—in the movie as well as all around us in our own lives—we end up believing in something we should be much too smart and much too grown up to believe in.

Intimacy for Men 101

Since this will be an intensive five week course and since I recognize that intimacy is a brand new subject for many of you, I promise to proceed slowly and to answer any questions that might come up along the way. I knew a creative writing teacher once who began her course by congratulating her students for showing up and thereby taking the first essential step on the long road to becoming a poet or playwright. So, too, with this course. Congratulations, you have all taken the first step on the long road to becoming more caring, more open men.

Yes, we have a question already. That's right, you in the back, with the tattoo and the copy of *Hustler*. Right, the fellow wearing the "Bowlers Do It in the Gutter" T-shirt. What's that? You want to know what makes me such a quote, unquote expert on intimacy? That is, of course, a legitimate question and if you will just bear with me for a little while longer, I'll answer it. In the meantime, let's review the course outline.

Week One: What is Intimacy?
This session will provide an historical overview of male intimacy. Class discussion will focus on how men have expressed their emotions and communicated their feelings to their girlfriends, wives and significant others from ancient times to the present.
This will be a short session.

After a break we will discuss how much money each of us earns, whether the Canadiens are going to make the playoffs and what's for dinner. Then we'll all go bowling.

Supplementary texts: *Cosmopolitan, The Myth of Male Power: Why Men are the Disposable Sex,* and *The Basics of Bowling.*

Week Two: Huh?

Listening is the cornerstone of intimacy and a fundamental part of any successful relationship. Pretending to listen is, however, a good backup plan. In this session, the class will be encouraged to do the former while practicing the latter, just in case.

That way, if you can't listen because you have other, more pressing matters on your mind—bowling, for instance—you will work on remembering a key word in each sentence. That way when you are asked later, as you undoubtedly will be, "Have you even heard a single word I said?" you can answer honestly and say, "I sure did." (FYI: the same principle does not apply to apologizing. Do not bother looking for loopholes. Saying, "I'm sorry you feel that I might have done something which in some way might have upset you," is not an actual apology and women can no longer be fooled into thinking it is. You will only have to apologize again. Remember, love does not mean never having to say you're sorry. Love means having to say you're sorry as often as possible.)

Supplementary reading: *You Just Don't Understand: Women and Men in Conversation* and *10 Secrets of Bowling.*

Week Three: Happy Talk

Remember the movie *Cool Hand Luke*? Remember when the warden of the chain gang says to Paul Newman, "what we have here is a failure to communicate," and then, a little later, Paul Newman is shot dead? Well, this is just one of the reasons why communication is such an essential skill in our daily lives. In a relationship, it's also important to remember that men and women have very different methods of communicating.

Generally speaking, women practice what is called "face-to-face intimacy". This means if they believe a man is acting like a big, dumb jerk they will usually let him know how they feel by saying, "You are such a big dumb jerk!" Men who, generally speaking, practice "side-by-side intimacy" will often be puzzled by this kind of direct approach and will often respond by saying, "Are you talking to me?" or "What did I do now?"

Simply put, the problem comes down to a lack of practice and experience. While men engage in "side-by-side intimacy" every day with their buddies—showing affection by punching one another on the shoulder—they are less apt to practice "face-to-face intimacy." As a class exercise, we will all turn our desks around and stare at each other until we can think of something honest and caring to say to each other. This exercise will be continued into Week Four and Five, if necessary. It will account for twenty-five percent of your grade.

Sorry, is your hand up? That's right, you in the back. What's that? You still want to know what makes me such a goddamn, hotshot, quote, unquote expert on intimacy? Once again, good question, but can we save it for later?

Week Four: Putting the Glow Back in the Afterglow

Using overhead projectors and audio-visual aids, the class will deal with the sometimes controversial issue of how long a man is required to stay awake and cuddle following sex. While some experts say a couple of minutes, tops, others say that these days you better be prepared to stay up all night if you know what's good for you. This is, of course, a trick question. My own independent studies reveal that you should cuddle until you accidentally pin your lover's hair to the bed with your elbow. Don't worry, you'll know when this happens.

Fortunately, medical science may make this entire debate irrelevant. Right now, exciting research is being conducted on the hormone oxytocin, also referred to as "the cuddle chemical." Commonly found in pregnant women, oxytocin stimulates the contractions of the uterine muscle and the secretion of milk. It is believed to be an important factor in a mother bonding with her child.

The implications for men are obvious. If oxytocin can be isolated and injected into or ingested by the bonding-challenged male, human relationships, as we know them, will change forever. Studies are still in the early stages, but there are already rumors that male laboratory rats on heavy doses of oxytocin are nineteen times more likely to open up about their problems after a hard day at the maze. One female specimen was overheard saying that she hardly recognized the old rat any more.

Week Five: The Crying Game

This session will be dedicated to debunking the popular myth that men don't cry, a myth that even condom manufacturers are perpetuating, as this recent magazine ad demonstrates: "Ramses provides both strength and sensitivity with that exquisite natural feel. Now all you need to do is learn to cry."

This is nonsense. Men know how to cry. Anyone who has seen a professional athlete in the last few years win some championship, set a record, retire or be sued for sexual harrassment knows that men don't have to take a back seat to any woman when it comes to sobbing openly in public.

But what is sometimes overlooked when women, in particular, complain about how men never cry is that there's usually nothing we'd like to do more. Speaking for myself, if I cried every time I felt like it I'd never be able to go bowling. And even if I did, my eyes would be red and puffy and the other guys on my team would notice and I'd never hear the end of it.

The trouble is that women mistakenly think men feel about crying the way Superman feels about Kryptonite—that it will render us vulnerable and impotent. Not surprisingly, men don't really mind having women think this, since it keeps us from having to acknowledge all the other things that we worry will render us impotent. The other reason we don't cry is that we don't want to be perceived as being as sappy and sentimental as most professional athletes these days.

Class Assignment: We will watch television commercials for Hallmark greeting cards, long distance telephone services, and The Church of Jesus Christ of Latter Day Saints.

I believe that covers everything. There will be no seating arrangement: men need to learn to be more spontaneous. There will be no attendance either: I don't want you here if you really don't want to be. Students will be graded on a curve, an extremely wide curve. There will be extra credit for crying in class. In the last week, the class will be encouraged to share their true feelings about the course. You will be encouraged to explain why it was good for you.

Now, are there any questions? Yes, you in the back with the tattoo.

Fetish Fever

Alfred Kinsey, a bow-tied, former Eagle Scout from New Jersey and the first person to do a statistical study of America's sexual habits, used to cruise Times Square, pick up hitchhikers and knock on stranger's doors just so he could ask them as many as five hundred and twenty-one questions about their sex lives. The results of his survey, when they first began to be published in 1948, shed light on a variety of subjects no one had wanted to talk or think about before. Kinsey's survey proved, for example, that homosexuality was not nearly as rare as some people wanted to believe and that women were not nearly as prim and proper as some other people wanted to believe. Needless to say, the general public was shocked.

A couple of years ago when the first comprehensive sex survey since Kinsey was completed and the results were released, the public was shocked again. This time, though, it was because no one wanted to believe that they were as boring as the survey was making them sound. Who could have guessed that "the second most appealing sex act"—after intercourse—was watching one's partner undress? People all across the country were all thinking the same thing: "I thought we were a lot weirder than that."

I thought so too—at least judging by how trendy fetishes have become nowadays. While it's true that there was a time when a fetish was, almost by definition, the sort of thing you preferred to keep to yourself, that time has come and gone.

Now, there are fetish cafes and emporiums and conventions. Thanks to the videos of Madonna, the artist formerly known as Prince and others, people who literally get off on leather and whips are part of mainstream culture—perceived to be no kinkier than philatelists or spelunkers.

Not far from where I live there's a nightclub which holds a "fetish night" once a month. In the classified sections of respectable newspapers and magazines, you can find a toll-free number to call for an erotic bath from "a Daddy figure." Or you can order "Used Panties" by mail. Prices start at twenty-five dollars. Which is the kind of markup even my late grandfather, a grocery store owner who was always complaining about his overhead, couldn't have found fault with.

No one has to be ashamed any more and, more to the point, no one is. These are the 1990s, not the 1890s. We live in an age in which confession is not only considered good for the soul, but in which confessing to some deep, dark secret will guarantee you your fifteen minutes of fame. By the end of the twentieth century, it's a safe bet that all of us will have been booked on *Geraldo* or be referred to by name on the front page of *The National Enquirer* at least once.

But trash TV and tabloid headlines are not the only places where the dirt is being dished. Last year, in the prestigious and usually discreet *New Yorker* magazine, Daphne Merkin, a long-time contributor and self-described "conscientious Upper East Side mother," confessed to a lifelong predilection for playing the title role in her own version of "Spanking the Maid." In a critically acclaimed autobiography, a distinguished poet and Princeton professor admitted to having sex with his dog when he was a young man. (Rumor has it that the dog has already been contacted by an agent.) In the best newspapers as well as the worst, Prince Charles has said that the highest goal to which he aspires is not to be the next monarch of England but to be a tampon.

Even masochists these days seem to be brimming with self-confidence and self-esteem. On the radio recently, I heard a young woman become indignant when she was asked if she was ashamed of her desire to be tied up. "Why should I be?" she said, proud of her need to be dominated and humiliated.

Personally, I'm glad people are no longer bashful about their kinky behavior because, let's face it, there's really nothing for them to be bashful about any more. There probably never was. Only nitwits and teenagers honestly believe that there is something they and their lovers can do that's somehow new. Human beings have been around for millions of years and considering that the O.J. Simpson trial only lasted for a little over twelve months, we've spent a good percentage of that time having to make our own fun. So trust me on this: everything's been done before. Not only that, everything's been done twice, right side up, upside down, wearing vinyl, wearing latex, wearing polyester, with a whip, with whipped cream, with shaving cream, with spumoni ice cream.

To be honest, it's the people without a fetish to call their own who are starting to feel a little bashful and a little out of the loop these days. People like me. In my case, though, it's not as if I haven't thought about other options—about ways to be more kinky.

I considered voyeurism first. Given my television viewing habits, which some might already characterize as perverse, I figured watching other people have sex would seem like an obvious option for me. I can understand the thrill of having a front-row seat as other people perform for your benefit, but I can also see my reduced attention span and my fondness for channel surfing turning into a problem. I can practically hear myself asking, "How much longer do you two think you'll be doing that?"

S & M was next. A genuine possibility, I thought. Who doesn't like to be in control, in command? But when I fell apart removing a splinter from a girlfriend's finger, I realized that while I didn't mind inflicting guilt on a loved one, physical pain was another matter.

With the "S" ruled out, there was still the "M" to consider. But if my normal reaction to stubbing my toe is any indication of how well I deal with pain, I'm worried that the moment my partner began to attach a viselike clip, let's say, to my left nipple, I'd be hopping around the room like Jerry Lewis. Honestly, I don't see how that is going to put even the most dedicated dominatrix in the mood.

Exhibitionism? Too drafty.

Menage-à-trois? Too crowded.

Hot wax? Too hot.

Necrophilia? Too dead.

Tranvestitism? Obviously, you haven't seen my legs.

Props, that's my real problems with all these activities. They require too many props and too much preparation. From what I can tell, dedicated fetishists also take themselves much too seriously.

Not long after we first became lovers a girlfriend and I broke her bed at a particularly inopportune and delicate moment and while my initial reaction was to be extremely pleased with myself, my next reaction was to suppress my laughter. I was trying my best not to lose my, well, let's call it concentration. "Don't make me laugh," I warned her. But she was already giggling uncontrollably.

A moment later, as the two of us, naked and sweaty and a little frustrated, began arguing about how to prop up the twisted leg, we both realized how ludicrous the whole situation was. I do wonder, however, if we'd gone to the additional trouble of hooking up pulleys and chains and outfitting ourselves in all kinds of paraphernalia whether we would have still been able to enjoy the luxury of laughing at ourselves. Maybe not, which would have been a shame since a shared joke allows for a kind of intimacy between two people that will last a lot longer than any orgasm. Speaking strictly for myself, I'd like to say here and now that if I ever do show up in the bedroom wearing a leather harness and carrying a riding crop, I expect whatever woman I'm with to fall on the floor laughing. I wouldn't respect her if she didn't.

Maybe it's just that this whole burgeoning fetish industry seems like gilding the lily to me. I have a difficult time thinking of sex as an activity that needs to be embellished with elaborate costumes and scripts. The question I keep asking myself is: "Why would anyone prefer playing a role to just playing?"

I suppose the answer is obvious. It's because intimacy is terrifying and hard. It's a lot safer and a lot easier to be excited by an object—or by a person you insist on treating like an object—than by an actual ambiguous human being. "The desires of the human heart are crooked as a corkscrew," W.H. Auden said and he was right. Love has always been kinky enough for me.

There are mornings, lying in bed with a woman I love, after we've just had sex, when I think: "Why does anyone ever bother doing anything else?" Later, walking together on the street or having lunch in a restaurant I always have a problem getting over how mundane our behavior is at that moment compared to all the things we were doing just a little while earlier. I feel like a double agent, entrusted with secret information. I can't help feeling that everyone is staring at us and it's all I can do to keep from blushing or even winking at strangers.

I used to think this sort of behavior was a sign of immaturity on my part, but I'm not so sure any more. Maybe it just takes a much more sophisticated or a much more jaded person than me not to feel as overwhelmingly giddy about sex as I usually do. I even get a kick out of watching my partner undress.

Virtually Sex

Maybe, I'm just slow to pick up on these things, but there seems to be another sexual revolution going on and no one even had the courtesy to tell me. No one called. No one faxed. No one tried to reach me by e-mail. Or contacted my website. What's wrong with me anyway?

Sorry if I seem a little touchy about this subject, but I have a reason. You see, I missed the last sexual revolution altogether. I'd just entered puberty in 1969, the year of Woodstock, so I guess if I wanted to I could have participated in "the summer of love." I could have been getting high and cavorting in the mud with free-spirited, naked young women. Instead, I was in my next door neighbor's dark, musty basement, playing a board game called Strat-O-Matic in which dice and computerized cards are used to simulate a major league baseball game. In my own defense, Strat-O-Matic is surprisingly authentic. My neighbor and I not only played a twenty-four team, one hundred and sixty-two game schedule, we kept complete and thorough statistics. We were as busy as accountants at tax time. We were geeks, in other words.

Indeed, all through high school I took a lot of pride in the fact that I never yielded to peer pressure. As a consequence, I didn't smoke, drink, do drugs or indulge in uninhibited, meaningless sex with strangers. And by the time I'd turned seventeen the question I couldn't help asking myself was: what's so bad about peer pressure anyway? Which is why I think I should at least know what I am missing before the latest sexual revolution passes me by.

Not much, as it happens. This time around everyone seems to be far too busy talking about sex to actually have it.

When I say talk I primarily mean talk radio. On just about every stop on the dial, at just about any time of the day, you can find a psychologist or therapist or some other self-proclaimed know-it-all inducing strangers to call in and reveal their most intimate secrets.

Fran Lebowitz was right: "Spilling your guts is just exactly as charming as it sounds." The chatter about premature ejaculation and multiple orgasms is unrelenting and, worst of all, it comes, so to speak, without warning. Unlike movies or television, radio talk shows don't have any system in place to alert unsuspecting listeners that what they are about to hear might make them cringe.

For instance, I was in the corner store the other evening when a woman's voice came over the speaker system. She was discussing her G-spot, how her husband had finally located it, and how the result was, by her admittedly unscientific estimate, a bucket measuring a half gallon of bodily fluid. She was just calling to ask if this was normal.

There were a couple of other customers in the store—all men—and we were staring at our feet as if our feet knew something about G-spots that we didn't. We kept our heads down as we all walked, practically single file, out of the store. I was the last in line and the clerk apologized to me, explaining how his employer didn't want anyone, under any circumstances, changing the channel on the radio. Before I left, I muttered, "Make an exception."

Put another way, you can have, as the woman with the bucket found out, too much of a good thing. Take the following example—*Warning: Some readers may find this excerpt offensive, potentially icky and, most important of all, none of their damn business. I know I do. Reader discretion is advised*—of an actual exchange transcribed from a local program about sex:

Radio Therapist: All right, now we have Bill on the line. Thanks for calling and tell us, Bill, what can we help you with tonight?

Caller: My wife says I'm extremely well endowed and she can't get enough of my penis and the problem is all she wants to do is perform fellatio. When it comes to lovemaking she just wants to do it once a night and that's it. She'll perform oral sex all night long.

Radio Therapist: And what exactly is your problem again?

All right, the therapist didn't say that, but he might have. I can't say for sure what his reply was because I turned off the radio before Bill was finished. One reason was because listening to these call-in shows is like reading the letters in *Penthouse*. Your initial impulse is not to believe a single sentence anyone says. Your second impulse is not to believe a single word. Besides, the more you listen the more difficult it becomes to distinguish between the people who are genuinely screwed up and those who are just screwed up enough to discuss their sex lives on the radio.

I suppose it's too late by now to argue that I'm no prude. Because, it's true, listening to most of this stuff makes me blush. It's true, too, that I've been known to cover my eyes during the sex scenes in movies.

But what does that prove, except that there is a law of diminishing returns, a point at which more does become less? In 1929 James Thurber and E.B. White wrote a book called *Is Sex Necessary?* and in the preface they complained about "the flood of books" by sociologists, psychologists and analysts all out to make sex what it never has been and never will be: understandable. As far as our interest in sex goes, nothing much has changed in the last seventy years or the last seventy thousand. All that's happened is that our access to information about sex has grown exponentially. It's too bad information is not a virtue all by itself; too bad it's not wisdom either. And what's really too bad is that we don't know that by now.

I suppose anyone who suspected I was a prude before is convinced after this little tirade. Which reminds me of something else that bothers me about all these so-called sex experts—they are insufferably self-important. I wouldn't mind them nearly as much if they just admitted they are talking dirty, because people sometimes like to listen to dirty talk and leave it at that. Instead, they insist they are providing an essential public service and that if listeners didn't find out about multiple orgasms and anal sex from them, we just wouldn't have a clue. But there's a flaw in this argument and it's that this kind of information is not just available everywhere, it's unavoidable. The mainstream media is overloaded with it. Even *Reader's Digest* routinely offers a condensed list of sex secrets.

But the real problem I have with all the endless advice and analysis on the radio and elsewhere is the notion that we are now capable of figuring out what has been confusing human beings since the beginning of time. No, I don't think you have to be a prude to think that candor has given way to license, that talk isn't only cheap, it is cheapening what is perhaps the only genuine mystery human beings still share.

"You can't remember sex," E.L. Doctorow once wrote. "You can remember the fact of it and recall the setting, and even the details, but the sex of the sex cannot be remembered, the substantive truth of it....is by nature self-erasing....there is no memory of it in the brain, only the deduction that it happened and that it passed, leaving you with a silhouette that you want to fill in again." In other words, some silhouettes can't be filled. Some questions were never intended to be answered.

Ironically, it was a caller to yet another radio talk show about sex in the nineties that made this point clear to me. His name was Louis and he was responding to an interview the host, a perky young woman, was conducting with a university professor about cybersex and teledildonics, which, I'm guessing, is more or less what you think it is.

Louis was taking their conversation far too seriously and he sounded inconsolable. He was worried, he said, about the impact that all this emphasis on virtual screwing in the place of actual screwing will have on natural selection and the future of the human race.

As Louis went on complaining about how we've gone too far, I could imagine the host and her guest rolling their eyes. Louis was the worst possible caller—a killjoy. Eventually, the host brushed him off with a polite but terse, "thanks for calling," and returned to the professor to discuss intercourse on the internet.

The message was clear, to me anyway. The world is divided into two kinds of people: those, like Louis, who believe when it comes to sex there is such a thing as too much information and those who believe you can never have enough. And though it seems, more and more, like the second kind are taking over, until they do, I'm with Louis.

The Penis: A Troubleshooting Guide

Not long after Lorena Bobbitt used a filleting knife to separate her husband from his manhood, I heard Naomi Wolf, the best-selling feminist author, warn women, particularly those who seemed unable to contain their laughter after the incident had been widely reported and the trial televised, that maybe this was not a cause for celebration after all. "The penis is our friend," she told a radio interviewer, and you could almost hear the collective sigh of relief from all the male listeners in the audience.

Sure, the remark was condescending. Yes, it sounded as if we were having our heads, so to speak, patted. But at a time when penis envy has been replaced by penis enmity, when phallocentric is the one thing you don't want to be and when the male member is viewed in politically correct North American society as either an instrument of torture or a poor substitute for a turkey baster, you can't blame a guy for being grateful that someone finally has something nice to say in public.

Too grateful at the time to point out how unlikely it was for this woman—indeed, for any woman—to understand what it means to be responsible for such a fickle and fundamentally willful part of the anatomy. For men, the care and maintenance of our private parts is a constant source of concern. From Calvin Klein underwear to condoms, entire industries and advertising campaigns have sprung up to shelter the male organ from harm. Boxer shorts and athletic supporters were invented just to keep it secure and comfortable. Still, no matter how much we try to placate it, it remains as restless as a two year old—never content in one place, always requiring adjustment.

Women generally see the penis at its best, hopeful and up for a good time. What women don't realize is that the rest of the time it is not quite so gregarious and fun-loving. John Updike compared having a penis to being in charge of a "demon of sorts...whose errands seem, at times, ridiculous. It is like having a (much) smaller brother toward whom you feel both fond and impatient."

My feelings are even more ambivalent. My penis is, in other words, no friend of mine. At best, we've been able to establish a love-hate relationship over the years. But ever since something white, sticky and unexpected emerged from it one night while I was sleeping, I've stopped trying to figure out what it's up to. I just assume it has a mind of its own.

Men are often accused of thinking with their penises. This isn't true. In reality, our penises are flying solo, doing all their thinking without us, like tiny—well not that tiny—tin-pot dictators. And because we never know what they're going to do next, men sometimes treat their penises with an inordinate amount of reverence—the way ancient savages, trying to ward off the next earthquake or volcano, kissed up to primitive gods—ascribing a kind of wisdom and supernatural power to the penis that it just doesn't possess in its daily humdrum existence.

Which is another point worth mentioning about men and their penises: whether we are bragging about our prowess or devastated by our lack of it, we tend to lose all sense of perspective and proportion. Keeping this in mind, I have at least tried to avoid doing what a lot of men do—personalize my penis and give it a cute name like Rover or Spike. (Incidentally, I have no problem with women giving it a cute name.) Still, I confess there have been occasions when I have commiserated with it, apologizing for the lack of action. Other times, I have had to reproach it with a stern "hey you" as in "hey you, behave yourself."

I'm reminded of the story of the young boy who after he had the phenomenon of the wet dream explained to him in his sex education class said, "Gee, you have to watch it all the time, don't you?"

You bet you do. For most of us, the penis will always be a stranger—as incomprehensible to us as our VCRs. Like your VCR, you'll never understand how it works, you'll never be able to program it to do what you want when you want, and it will be prone to let you down when you're counting on it most. It's probably revealing that with all the various terms of endearment I could use to refer to my thing, I still call it "my thing." Which is why I've included a few important facts every man needs to know, a sort of troubleshooting guide to your private parts:

Size doesn't matter.

Women will always tell you this. Believe them. If you can't— and naturally you can't—remember size, like most things, is relative. If this helps, remember that the elephant's penis is five feet long, which is roughly the same size as Ross Perot; the blue whale's penis is eight feet long, which is about a foot bigger than your average basketball player.

The erect penis assumes an angle of 140° to 160°, give or take a few degrees.

I read this in a book so, please, take my word for it. Don't try measuring the angle yourself. If you do, you can use a protractor. But do not, under any circumstances, use one of those compasses they were always handing out in high school geometry class—the one with points at both ends.

The male private parts are made up of much more than the penis, which is really just the front man.

There is an elaborate plumbing and reproductive system at work behind the scenes and, as a result, there are always numerous things going wrong. This is why it's always a good idea to know exactly where your prostate is. Then, when you find it, call me and let me know.

Accentuate the positive.

According to one study, nearly forty percent of women prefer chocolate to sex, according to another study fifty percent believe "a good night's sleep is better than sex." So why do we even bother? Because that still leaves ten percent unaccounted for.

The Sporting Life

So I'm watching what appears to be this new sport—topless rhythmic gymnastics—on television the other night and I'm asking myself the question I know most women would ask me if they could: "What is it with you guys and sports?" Most of the time women will excuse a man's practically automatic interest in a half-naked gymnast doing handsprings on a floor mat while throwing colored streamers in the air—an exhibition sport, if there ever was one—but they'll have a harder time understanding why we need to know how she's doing in the standings.

What can I say? We—meaning me in this case—get carried away. But then, most guys have the capacity to become completely immersed in athletic activities we wouldn't cross the street to watch. Thanks to cable TV, I am now well acquainted with the goofy intricacies of everything from miniature golf to synchronized swimming. I have a keen grasp of the rules of Australian Rules Football and I finally understand that the brooms in curling aren't used to tidy up.

Let's face it: as long as there is a color commentator in a bad blazer and a bad toupee describing the action and as long as there is a home team to root for, we're there. The home team doesn't even have to be from our home. The sport doesn't even have to be a real sport. I knew a guy once who became so involved in the game show *Family Feud* that when the family he'd arbitrarily decided to root for missed a no-brainer "Survey Says" answer, he booed them and kicked the coffee table across the room.

Ironically, both the stress and the joy of competition seem to be enhanced rather than diminished when someone else is doing the competing. We are all champions sitting on the couch, the remote control in one hand, a bag of pretzels in the other and a beer in the other.

I know, that's three hands. But before you start sending nasty notes to my editor, consider one thing: at this very moment Albert Cohen of Troy, New York, a man who will go down as a pioneer in CPR (Couch Potato Research), has invented the Hi-5, a mechanical arm, hand really, which is designed to slap you five in your own home, thereby allowing solitary sports fans to celebrate on-field achievements just as if they were really in the stands with the rest of the crowd or perhaps even on the field with the athletes. If the Hi-5 catches on, as it's certain to, it will solve one of the last remaining hurdles to being a content and fulfilled armchair athlete—artificial camaraderie.

The biggest problem, however, is the one I mentioned at the start and one that will be a lot tougher to get over: how do you explain all this to women? Frankly, I don't know. It's one of the mysteries of being male—this talent we have for living an enormous percentage of our lives vicariously. Sometimes, it's even a mystery to us.

Recently, a female friend teased me about my habit of referring to the local baseball team in the first person plural. As in: "Our starting pitching is fine, but we really have to improve our bullpen and our on-base average." "Our?" she said, mimicking me. "We?"

I didn't know how to respond, though I was tempted to repeat what Louis Armstrong said when a female admirer asked him to define jazz. "Lady," he said, "if you gotta ask, you ain't never going to know."

But why was I being so defensive? Perhaps because I suspect that behind all of women's teasing and bewilderment is the real issue: what do we care about more—the Stanley Cup Playoffs or them? I think I can speak for all men when I say that it's no contest: we care about women more. Really, we do. If it doesn't always seem that way it's only because we sometimes fall into the trap of making unfair comparisons between the two. Relationships, for example, require communication and sharing our feelings; hockey discourages it.

Here's a purely hypothetical story about a person I'll call Dumb Guy. On his way to watch the Super Bowl at a friend's house, Dumb Guy calls another friend to find out if he wants to come along. According to this second friend's wife, her husband has already gone out to watch the game and won't be back until much later. So Dumb Guy thanks her and says goodbye, but before he can hang up, his friend's wife starts flirting with him. He thinks it's harmless so he flirts back. Until she says something like, "Why don't you come over here instead? We can have a lot more fun."

Dumb Guy isn't dumb, he hears what he hears, but he still figures she is kidding so he says so. He calls her bluff. Which is when she says something like: "Why don't you just find out for yourself?"

Which is when Dumb Guy starts thinking that maybe she isn't kidding. He is faced with a dilemma. He starts weighing all the possibilities. She might not be serious after all and wouldn't that be embarrassing? But what if she is serious? Could he do it? Betray his friend? And while he's wrestling with all the ethical and moral issues that face him, he suddenly remembers it's Super Bowl Sunday. This is not the deciding factor, understand, but it tips the balance. He is supposed to be somewhere watching a football game. Not only that, it's the last one of the year. And this is how he ends up on the couch in some other guy's basement drinking beer and trying to convince himself that he is not dumb, not really. Some team beat some other team by forty-five points, his friend's wife eventually asked for a divorce and remarried, and Dumb Guy is still wondering what might have happened.

I'm not dumb either, but, in the same circumstances, I can't say for sure what I would have done. Casey Stengel used to say there are three things that can happen in baseball: "You can win or you can lose, or it can rain." Relationships are a lot more complicated than that. Anything can happen.

Of course, what most men really want is for everything to happen at the same time. We're childish in that way. Childish enough, in my case, to keep trying to teach whatever woman I'm involved with to enjoy watching baseball. But no matter how much they care about me, when they find out that there are one hundred and sixty-two games in a season and that most of them are played on warm summer nights, they will inevitably say: "You're kidding, right?"

Sometimes, though, things just fall into place. I can't remember ever being happier than the night a lover and I had passionate sex and then I accidentally—I swear it was an accident—rolled over on the remote control button and watched the Expos rally in the bottom of the ninth to beat the Phillies on a two-out double while I was holding my lover in my arms.

Can it get any better than this? I remember thinking. Well, yes it can and it will. As soon as I buy my own Hi-5 mechanical hand and set it up to slap me five after the game is over.

RELATIONSHIPS

"Love is strange and true love is strange but true."
—Josephine Humphreys

Is Everybody Happy?

The first question that occurred to me when the Queen of England announced that she'd had an "annus horribilus" was the question that always occurs to me first: how does this affect me? I know what you're thinking: what could Elizabeth II and I possibly have in common?

Nothing, as it turns out. I had a pretty good year.

Actually, it was better than that. It was great. The truth? Two words: annus wonderfulus.

I recognize this puts me in an untenable position. Even now, as I recall how I fell in love or how I finally found boxers shorts that don't ride up on me, I have to remind myself not to smile when I'm out in public. That's because I've learned a valuable lesson about being happy: it's no piece of cake. And, frankly, I'm just not sure I can keep it up. Which explains why optimism, like some forms of insanity, is temporary.

For starters, you can't ever be cranky or cynical. You are obliged to believe only the best of people—that Lucien Bouchard doesn't really want to break up the country, that Madonna will be a wonderful mom.

You wouldn't think so, but a lot of effort goes into a sunny disposition. There is even a book out specifically aimed at helping those of us who are happy remain that way. Like people on a diet, we require a maintenance program. In *How to Be Happier Day by Day,* Alan Epstein, Ph.D., offers—along with "a money-back happiness guarantee"—three hundred and sixty-five practical suggestions:

2 May—Take a nap in the afternoon.
13 June—Do something without your clothes on.
15 September—Eat popcorn for dinner.
31 December—Think about your purpose in life.

"Pleasure chews and grinds us," Montaigne said, and though he never got a Ph.D., he was right. Like everything else nowadays, happiness is stressful. Trust me, you don't know what pressure is until you've gotten up each morning, prepared to mope and complain, just like you always have, only to realize that you can't make it stick any more. No one will listen. You'll be ignored.

Don't try telling anyone how happy you are either, since it's a safe bet that they're not and they'll resent you until the day they die. On the off chance they think they're doing just fine, thanks very much, it's a sure thing that when you tell them how much better you're doing, they'll become depressed and resent you even more.

Of course, the worst thing about being happy is that it can't last. Laugh too much and you'll cry later, my mother used to say, not just repeating a family motto but expressing a law of the universe as immutable as gravity: everything that goes up must come down.

Remember this: no one is wrong more often than an optimist. If you need proof, just think of all the people standing in line to buy a lottery ticket every week—people who haven't figured out yet that their chances of winning (about thirteen million to one) are virtually the same whether they purchase a ticket or not.

Don't get the wrong idea: I am not unusually cranky nor am I one of those people who suffer from anhedonia, otherwise known as "the psychological condition characterized by the inability to experience pleasure in normally pleasurable acts." I don't mind being happy. I could even learn to like it. And that's what worries me.

Woody Allen, whose working title for *Annie Hall* was *Anhedonia*, said that life is divided into two categories: the miserable and the horrible. Consider yourself lucky, he added, if you're just miserable.

Anton Chekhov had an even more practical suggestion. "There ought to be behind the door of every happy, contented man someone standing with a hammer continually reminding him with a tap that there are unhappy people; that however happy he may be, life will show him her laws sooner or later, trouble will come for him."

So what are people in a good mood supposed to do? Snap out of it. The trouble is that this is often easier said than done.

There just aren't a lot of research dollars being raised to solve the problems of the chronically happy. There are no telethons, no fund-raising campaigns, no government grants. What we have, in other words, is a problem in desperate need of attention. That's why I've decided to volunteer to go back to school to get a Ph.D. of my own, and write a book called *How to Be More Miserable Day by Day.* And just in case you're already worrying about the perils of being an incurable optimist, here's a preview:

2 May—Take a nap in the afternoon.

13 June—Do something without your clothes on.

15 September—Eat popcorn for dinner.

31 December—Think about your purpose in life.

I don't know about you, but I'm feeling worse already.

Role Models

It's encouraging these days to know that even people with inherited problems—from the children of alcoholics to the children of shopaholics—can find a 12-step program to address their needs. And, as anyone involved in a 12-step program will tell you, the first step to recovery is admitting you have a problem. So here's my confession: My name is Joel Y. and I am the product of a happy family.

I know what you're thinking: how does anyone survive an ordeal like that? Especially today, when, according to most self-respecting self-help experts, 96% of families are dysfunctional? Let me tell you, it's not easy.

It's not easy to talk about all this either. For as long as I can remember, I have lived a lie—pretending I was as messed up by my childhood as everyone else I knew. But I can't pretend any more. Perhaps because I know that, like me, there are lots of other people out there who have had to come to terms with the realization that it is no picnic being functional.

Did your father teach you to play hockey, but never put pressure on you to be the next Wayne Gretzky? Did your mother always remember to pick you up after school? Were your parents fond of each other? If the answer to all of these questions is yes, you probably qualify for the support group I'm thinking of starting called Adult Children of Parents Who Were Kind of Nice to Them. Or ACPWKNT. Of course, I'll have to work on the acronym if I ever hope to earn a guest spot on *Oprah*—you know, the show they haven't done yet about reasonably well adjusted people who lead reasonably well adjusted lives. How about the Society for Adults who are Pleased with their Parents? SAPP, for short.

In the meantime, I'm not holding my breath waiting for Oprah's people to call. I know that the cross I have to bear is not one that is in vogue at the moment and not one that is inherently dramatic. Even so, it has presented some special problems for a person in my line of work. Being a writer and not having a disastrous childhood to fall back on for material is like being a bullfighter without a bull. You can wave your red cape around all you want, but no one is going to take you seriously. "They fuck you up, your Mum and Dad," the poet Philip Larkin famously said. But what if they don't? What is there to write about then?

I remember a few years ago I needed to create a traumatic childhood experience for the main character in a novel I was working on and the best I could come up with from my own life was being locked out of the house. The more I thought about the incident, though, the more convinced I became that it hadn't happened. I never was locked out of the house. How could I have been? Someone was always home.

Today, everyone—from teachers to social workers to politicians—is expressing legitimate concern about the long term effects that being raised in day care centres will have on a generation of children. Likewise, there's no shortage of theories about the impact, especially on male children, of being raised by single mothers and of not having a father or father figure around. Listen to all the dire predictions and you can't help feeling that the best that these young boys can hope for is to grow up to be uncommunicative and unfeeling. At worst…well, does the name Jeffrey Dahmer ring a bell?

But no one seems to be worrying about the long term effects on people like me whose mother and father were always around. Actually, I didn't have just one parent to come home to but two. My father was a sign painter, a freelancer at a time when every other man in the neighborhood left for his job early in the morning and came home well into the evening.

Their children, even their wives, seldom had a clear idea of what they did or where they were during the day. But I always knew exactly where my father was. He was at home. And my mother was with him. I don't remember having a house key until I was twenty. Why would I have needed one?

I also don't remember ever hearing my parents fight in front of me or even raise their voices to each other. The worst thing I can recall is that my father would tease my mother mercilessly. One of his favorite stories was about a customer who came to the house to pick up an order. The man stayed to chat for a while and spent all of that time remarking on how attractive my mother was. He went on and on, irritating my father and delighting my mother. She kept looking over at my father, as if to say, "I hope you're listening to all this because if you're not I'm going to repeat it all later." Eventually, the customer rose to leave and walked straight into a very large and very visible beam in the middle of our basement.

Every family creates its own myths and my father loved to tell and retell this story, always embellishing it a little more each time, until it was impossible to be sure of what happened and what didn't. After a few years what really happened didn't matter anyway. All that mattered was the look on my father's face, which became redder and redder, and the sound of his laughter, which became more and more out of control the closer he came to delivering the punch line. The one about my mother's ardent admirer turning out to be as blind as Mr. Magoo.

For her part, my mother pretended to be bothered by the story, which only added to my father's pleasure in retelling it. A good sport, she played along. This was an unusual dynamic in their relationship. Usually, my father followed her lead. That had been true from the start. At first, her parents had objected to her marrying my father because he had contracted polio as a boy, walked with a pronounced limp and wore an iron brace on his paralyzed right leg. My mother's parents liked him well enough, but they wondered if he would be able to support their daughter and a family—or even have a family. My father, who had good reason to feel sorry for himself and who was, as a result, more often crippled by self-pity than by polio, was hurt by their doubts about him, but he wasn't angry. How could he be? He had the exact same doubts about himself.

I really don't think he would have married my mother if she hadn't insisted that they ignore what other people—her own parents included—had to say. In this regard, she saved him. Something she would do again and again. It was her decision, for example, that he become a sign painter so he would be able to work at home. It was her decision, too, for us to leave the city and buy a house in the suburbs.

My mother died when I was twenty, my father died almost two years later, so I never really had the opportunity to observe their relationship as an adult and compare it to relationships of my own. Instead, I can only speculate on how I think it worked and, yes, create myths of my own. There's a controversial psychological term called "false memory syndrome" in which people supposedly focus on the bad things that happened to them when they were growing up and, as an adult, remember these incidents as far worse than they were. My problem is the opposite one: I focus on the good things and remember them as far better than they were. I remember them as idyllic; I suffer from a sort of false memory lane syndrome.

I also can't help being attracted to women who don't mind being teased mercilessly and whom I can count on to have more confidence in me than I often have in myself. That's my curse, the curse of the SAPP. Understand, I'm not complaining, I'm just wondering when Oprah and her people will finally get around to calling.

Don't You Step on My Elevator Shoes

This is just a hunch, but I think the real reason H. Ross Perot dropped out of the U.S. presidential race in 1992 was because of his height. He just couldn't stand up, so to speak, to the inevitable barrage of short jokes. Even when he re-entered the race in the final month, commentators, pundits and late night comics were ready and waiting. David Letterman's number one reason for Perot's comeback—lower podiums.

The guy never had a chance.

Which probably worked out for the best in H. Ross's particular case. Still, I couldn't help feeling a twinge of sympathy for the pintsized billionaire.

Statistics don't lie. When it comes to elections or securing a date for the high school prom, height is destiny: the taller candidate invariably wins. No one knows this better than the Richlee Shoe Company. North America's leading manufacturer of elevator footwear, Richlee has been making "men taller since 1939." And, as they explain in their Christmas mail order catalogue, sales continue to "grow" at an amazing rate:

"Why? Because....surveys have shown that being taller has distinct advantages in business and social situations."

Of course, this raises a troubling sociological question— namely, what am I doing with an elevator shoe catalogue? Christmas shopping, just browsing, you know, for a tiny friend...

All right, I admit it: the catalogue is mine.

I guess I should have made this confession earlier, but I'm probably not as tall as you think I am. For that matter, I'm not as tall as I think I am. Not even as tall as it says I am on my driver's license.

In short, I'm short. And always have been. While promises were made to me when I was a boy that this would be a temporary problem—"You're going to shoot up," my mendacious relatives assured me at my bar mitzvah—it's turned out to be a lifelong condition. The only thing I have to look forward to now is shrinking.

Despite that, when I started to write about my size—or lack of it—I assumed it would be funny. Being short, I now realize, is no laughing matter.

Actually, this realization came to me a while ago. That's when a woman I had been pursuing for some time finally admitted that the real reason our relationship couldn't progress beyond the platonic stage was because she preferred taller men. Taller than her, she meant.

"But we're exactly the same size," I protested, taking out my driver's license to show her.

She just shrugged and glanced down at me sympathetically.

I was in denial—deep in it. But then, lying about your height comes naturally to short guys. Alan Ladd was 5'10" on the movie screen; he was 5'4" everywhere else. J. Edgar Hoover sat behind an elevator desk which would ascend whenever a G-Man over 5'7" entered the room. The latest revelations about Hoover's personal life haven't surprised me either—high heels and a bouffant hairdo are sizable temptations for a short man.

But if short men lie about their height, society drives us to it. We are viewed as cute and harmless—feisty at best. At a time when everyone is hypersensitive about not offending the newest, trendiest minority group, short guys—or The Vertically Challenged—remain fair game. We have no support groups, no 12-step program, no Short Guy Hotline to call.

There's another reason why we lie about our height—women. Women are nearly as superficial about a man's height as men are about women in general. Just check out the "Personals" column some time: the one quality women consistently demand from a prospective partner is height. And, remember, these are women who are otherwise blithely indifferent to sadomasochistic tendencies.

Some years ago, Sandy Allen, then the tallest woman in the world—7' 7 1/4" according to *The Guinness Book of World Records*—confessed that she'd never marry a smaller man. "I just have the idea the man should be bigger," she said.

So, yes, I ordered the elevator shoe catalogue. What choice did I have? Desperate times require desperate measures.

I'm pleased to report, however, that this story has a happy ending. I haven't sent away for my pair of shoes yet. That's mainly because the woman I'd been pursuing transcended her heightism. Now, she's put away her heels and cheerfully clips out newspaper articles about the latest trend in relationships: "Short Men and Tall Women—the Last Taboo." She cites statistical studies. According to one recent opinion poll done for *Oprah*, 87% of the people questioned did not object to taller women kissing shorter men in public. We've come a long way, baby.

Short guys are in. Already ecologically-friendly—we take up less space—we're also politically correct. According to one female psychologist, we just may be the only hope for the future:

"Women used to be attracted to big men because they could bring home meat and defend us against marauders. But now women would be less likely to be (bullied) by small partners.... So start giving your rewards to thoughtful little people. Hire them, dance with them, marry them.... We can reverse the current genetic trend and save the universe."

My thinking exactly.

Sex and the Single Parking Spot

This is going to sound sappy, but when I fall in love I feel like singing in public and, trust me, I'm the last person in the world who should feel that way. Even sappier is that my taste in these circumstances tends to run to show tunes. "I Could Have Danced All Night" and "I Feel Pretty" are particular favorites. I may as well be Fred Astaire, too—so overwhelming is my impulse to dance down a crowded avenue, twirling in public and clicking my heels together.

But what no one mentions about those first heady days of a new romance is how unstable, how shaky you can also feel. It's not that the excitement starts to fade, because it doesn't. The sex is great and getting better. The shot in the arm of sheer hopefulness that you are experiencing is immune to misgivings. She can do no wrong and, amazingly, neither can you. You are just plain giddy, but it's what accompanies the giddiness—an almost surreal self-awareness—that is sometimes surprisingly unsettling.

I was in an accident once in which my car spun out of control and ended up crashing into a fence and facing the wrong way on the highway. The whole thing couldn't have lasted more than a few seconds, but in those few seconds I had the sensation, as people involved in accidents sometimes do, of watching myself and thinking, "No, this can't be happening to me. This is too awful." Falling in love elicits the same reaction, but in reverse. I watch myself and think, "This can't be happening. This is too good."

Maybe that's why I'm always keeping an eye open for what can go wrong: not necessarily between my lover and me, but just in general. In the early stages of a relationship, my intuition is in overdrive anyway, my senses buzzing. I'm more alert to everything around me, including potential dangers. Like city buses careening out of control or rabid dogs or lone snipers.

Of course, being paranoid is no guarantee that people aren't really out to get you. I have reason to believe, for instance, that an entire municipality—the city of W., a traditionally sedate, well-off suburb not far from downtown Montreal—did its utmost to drive a wedge between my girlfriend and me.

Conspiracy theories have a momentum all their own. Mine begins one night when the woman I had been friends with for several years suddenly decided that we should be more than just friends. From my point of view, this qualified as extraordinarily good news since I'd already reached the same decision, only I'd reached it two years earlier. Still, that first night as our initial doubts about what we were doing inevitably gave way to more compelling urges, my girlfriend-to-be stopped abruptly and announced that she had to place a telephone call to City Hall—specifically the Public Security Department.

I like to think that I am as open-minded and non-judgmental as the next guy and I recognize that everyone has their own way of getting in the mood, but this still seemed curious to me. Was she suggesting that we needed the approval of the municipality before we made love? What exactly was going on here? Was this what Aldous Huxley had in mind when he wrote *Brave New World*?

"Don't start acting weird," she said. "I have to call because you're not a resident and because you're not permitted to park your car on the street overnight, that's all. I have to let Security know that you are here and that you are my guest."

And that's how the situation was handled for the next couple of weeks. Actually, parking during the day was turning out to be much more of a problem. After all, my girlfriend and I were just starting to get to know each other and though I was supposed to be going downstairs every two hours to put money in the meter, I was usually preoccupied and happily forgot more than once. The tickets were piling up.

Which is why it was a relief each night to be able to check in with the city, give them my license number—I never made this call, my girlfriend did; we were both sure I would start giggling and not be able to stop—and not have to think about parking until the next morning. The problem seemed resolved to everyone's satisfaction until one night an obviously bitter, unfulfilled bureaucrat on the other end of the line told my girlfriend, "Sorry, the owner of this car won't be able to park overnight any more. You've already registered that license number six times and six times is the limit for one guest per year."

I realize now that this wasn't personal, but that's not how it felt at the time. I couldn't help wondering if somehow City Hall disapproved of me. Had they found out that I was from a less affluent suburb than W.? Had they decided that my car was an eyesore and a drain on property values? I even began to suspect that a secret town meeting had been held and a vote on the issue had been taken, with the mayor and a sizable majority of aldermen passing an initial motion declaring that I wasn't good enough for my girlfriend and then a second motion banishing me.

My girlfriend's suggestion that I might be overreacting only made me suspicious of her too. She tried to reassure me— pointing out that the same rule applied to everyone, not just me, but I kept muttering to myself, "That's what they want you to think." I also began to understand why Oliver Stone's movies are so humorless. There's nothing funny about the government turning against you.

"Six times, that's it. That's all we get," I finally shouted, my head in my hands.

"There has to be a way around this," my girlfriend said, remaining calm.

"You mean we have to break up, don't you?" I was holding my breath.

"Well, we might be able to explore some other alternatives first."

Miss Mond was one of those alternatives. A legendary figure at city hall, Miss Mond oversees parking on the streets of W. with an iron fist. The stories may be apocryphal, but even I've heard them—the ones about people who had gotten on her bad side and who ended up with no other choice but to sell their cars. But my girlfriend was optimistic. She believed she could talk Miss Mond into letting me pay a nominal fee for an overnight parking spot. It seems Miss Mond had taken a liking to her. They had a long heart-to-heart a few years ago. That was the good news. The bad news was that my girlfriend seemed to remember that the heart-to-heart had been on the subject of relationships. Miss Mond had said, in effect, that men were more trouble than they were worth.

I showed up at her office anyway, with my car registration, my cheque book and all my considerable hopes riding on this appointment. It didn't start well.

"She is supposed to come in, not you. I told her so," Miss Mond said, referring to my girlfriend. Then she went on to deliver a long speech about how people today never pay attention and how you can talk until you are blue in the face and they still only do what is convenient for them.

"I can get her... I can get my girlfriend," I volunteered, already out of my chair. "I can go away and she can come back."

"Never mind," Miss Mond said. "We'll just have to do it this way."

She began pulling the necessary forms from her filing cabinet in a deliberate, menacing manner. After she was through taking down my personal information, she began asking questions about my girlfriend. Questions I assumed she already had the answers to. But she persisted anyway: "Her last name? Spell it? Her address? Phone number? Postal code?"

Postal code? How could I not know the postal code of the woman I loved? I was finished; we were finished. Either I could learn to use public transit—I grew up in the suburbs and I would be lost without my car—or I could be alone for the rest of my life. Both choices were equally unacceptable. But then just when it looked like Miss Mond was about to fix me with the kind of imperious frown that the powerful have used since the beginning of time to make subjects who are annoying them disappear, she rubber-stamped the application form.

"You did a lot better than most of the ones who come in here," she said. "Just the other day a young woman was asking for a permit for a man who had just moved in with her and she didn't know what he did for a living or even his last name. What is the world coming to?"

"I wish I knew, Miss Mond, I wish I knew," I said. It was all I could do to keep from reaching across her tidy desk and hugging her.

My faith in humanity restored, I drove back to my girlfriend's apartment to tell her the good news. Clearly, Miss Mond was incorruptible. I had no doubt City Hall had tried to get to her, but she couldn't be pushed around. As I found a place to park—an officially sanctioned one—right in front of my girlfriend's apartment building, I knew I had been lucky on this day. I also knew it was the kind of luck you would be a fool to take for granted.

Now or Never

Whoever said the universe is unfolding as it should never met my barber. Every summer he tries to talk me into shaving off my beard. "Too hot," he says, pointing to my chin, adjusting the chair hopefully. I nod, agree with him and say, "Maybe next time."

I've had this beard for twenty years, nearly half my life, which is why any decision to remove it is hardly a simple one. It would constitute a major upheaval—too major to undertake without a lot of pointless worry first.

That's the thing about change—even when it promises to be for the better, it never feels that way. "Every decision is a mistake," the poet Edward Dahlberg said. So we fret, make elaborate lists of pros and cons, nag our friends and loved ones for advice we'd never dream of following.

I know a woman who recently decided to lease a house with her significant other. Once the papers were signed she began having recurring dreams about a stranger breaking into her bedroom window. "What do you think it means?" she asked.

"Beats me," I replied, trying to be tactful. But the truth is, you don't have to be Sigmund Freud to figure that one out. While her conscious mind was voting for a new adventure, her subconscious was screaming for everything to be the way it used to be, for everyone's favorite consolation prize—the status quo.

Very few of us accept change gracefully. The other day I had lunch with a friend, a new father, who, after coffee, took a pipe out of his breast pocket, lit it, and began to smoke. Something I'd never seen him do before. He also talked expertly, unceasingly, about cervical dilation and breast pumps. And all the time I could see the panic in his eyes—the silent realization that his life was never going to be the same again.

I have another friend who finally sold his condominium two years after his divorce. Having looked at new places all over town and after discussing their merits with everyone he knew, he eventually rented an identical condominium one block away.

I understand the impulse. For most of my life, I have been what people used to call a confirmed bachelor and as such I feel compelled to do what no one else seems prepared to these days: put in a good word for being in a rut.

There is a reason why I always trim my beard with the same pair of scissors, why I will not eat toast unless it has been sliced diagonally, why I can only sleep on one side of the bed, and the reason is because if I didn't, if I made the slightest alteration, I know I wouldn't be able to face the uncertainty and chaos lurking beneath the surface of my life. "I've had very little experience in my life," the novelist E.L. Doctorow boasted. "In fact, I try to avoid experience. Most experience is bad."

Words to live by.

But I also know that we resist change at our peril. Take the always pertinent example of Elvis Presley. Here's a man who transformed the history of popular music, but who, as he grew older and heavier, couldn't stop wearing those sequinned, skintight white jump suits. If he had changed his wardrobe, if he had just visited a Memphis Portly Men's Shop and bought a pullover and stretchy slacks, I'm convinced he'd still be alive today. A prisoner of fame as well as high cholesterol snacks, Elvis never could face the fact that he just wasn't the man he used to be.

"We must believe in free will. We have no choice," Isaac Singer said and so I do. But I also check my horoscope daily; and, more and more, I believe my fate is in the hands of whoever's responsible for putting those tiny messages into fortune cookies.

The last one I got said: "There are big changes ahead for you, but you will be happy." Two years later, as if on cue, I fell in love. I was a brand new man, reborn, transformed forever. I didn't recognize myself any more. I began to consider things I'd never considered before: like global warming, the future of Canada, marriage, raising a family, smoking a pipe.

I even accompanied my new love to her low impact aerobics class, something I'd never done before and never considered doing. Surrounded by strangers in spandex, I thought, "This is new, this is different. I can handle this."

But then, as the workout cassette began to play and people began jumping up and down in unison, I remembered the promise I'd made to myself at the age of thirteen to never participate in any form of exercise that didn't require a ball. Even for a man in love, too much change, embraced too quickly, can be as dangerous as the bends. So I tiptoed around the woman doing jumping jacks beside me and sneaked out of the gym. As I left, I took note of the music playing. Elvis Presley singing "It's Now or Never."

Two for the Road

There are two critical stages in any new relationship. The first is when you realize that the pet name your partner has carefully and lovingly selected for you—always Snookums in my case, don't ask me why—is making your teeth hurt. The second is when you decide to travel together.

I should confess a bias first. I am not an enthusiastic traveller. I've never been off the continent and never longed to be.

Who am I kidding? I don't even like watching *National Geographic* specials on TV. It's always seemed obvious to me that if "being offended is a natural consequence of leaving the house," as famous homebody Fran Lebowitz said, leaving the city is really asking for trouble.

Unfortunately, it doesn't matter how much I say I don't want to travel, the women in my life always think I'm kidding. "Oh come on," they invariably say, "you'll have fun. See new places, meet new people."

Like broccoli or psychotherapy, travel has acquired the reputation of being good for you. It broadens the mind and enriches the spirit. In short, it has the capacity to make you a better person. And that's what worries me. Visit Paris, for example, and there's a chance you'll come home discussing the *oeuvre* of Jerry Lewis and sporting a beret. It's a slim chance, granted, but not one I'm prepared to take.

Simply put, travel is overrated. In my experience, "new places" have inadequate plumbing and cable TV. "New people" is just a euphemism for strangers.

Obviously, selective memory is a prerequisite for anyone determined to be a successful globetrotter. The first thing I hear from people back from a trip are horror stories about how they were robbed or groped by the locals. How their hotel room didn't have a bed. How they were bitten by a very large, as yet unidentified insect. How they got sick (surveys have shown that 62% of all travellers suffer from some physical ailment while travelling) or nearly killed. How they will never go anywhere again. But then a month later their slides are developed and they're on the phone to their travel agent, planning another trip. Even Columbus kept coming back. "Okay, so it's not China," he probably told Mrs. C., "but I really need to get away for a while."

I'm not immune to selective memory either. Several years ago, my sisters and I went to Los Angeles, then on to Disneyland. We hated every minute. A few weeks later, though, looking at a photograph of Goofy and me slow-dancing, we'd already started to reminisce nostalgically about our vacation.

That's because travel, like falling in love, is a fundamentally romantic delusion. In the end, you cherish the good things and disregard the bad. It has, in other words, absolutely no connection to reality.

Of course, if it's reality you're looking for, you can always take the car. Your first road trip with a woman you are in love with serves an essential function for any couple who plan to hold hands from coast to coast: it's a reminder that you are two separate people, two very separate people. You, for example, are the person who decides, unilaterally, to drive past the sign saying, "Last Rest Stop for 112 kilometres." Your partner is the person, legs tightly crossed, who will never let you forget it.

Learning to master the art of highway travel with your significant other is like learning to sleep—and I do mean sleep—with them. Be prepared: the strength of your commitment will be tested, all your idiosyncrasies revealed. You crack your knuckles; she smokes. You like listening to oldies on the radio; she prefers an all-news station. You always wear the same pair of Bermuda shorts when you're driving a long distance; she doesn't understand the significance of lucky shorts, especially ones that are lime green. Be prepared as well for all your most peculiar theories to be revealed. If you've always secretly believed that Oliver Stone really knows who assassinated JFK, then you'll end up on some interminable stretch of highway explaining all of Stone's theories in excruciating detail.

A friend of mine finally understood how her husband's mind works when, on a recent trip from Halifax to Vancouver, their rearview mirror fell off into her lap. She was driving at the time and decided to stop and have it fixed. Her husband insisted they keep going. "Anyone who can't drive without mirrors shouldn't be driving," he said. Then, thinking he was being helpful, he added: "Just tell me when you want to know what's behind you and I'll turn around." It wasn't very long after that trip that they split up.

I'm surprised more relationships don't end on the road. If men and women were meant to be stuck together in a vehicle for longer than thirty minutes, she wouldn't keep pointing out the scenery and he wouldn't keep pointing out the variety of dead animals strewn across the highway. Every man I know has the same story—about the time the woman he was with demanded he pull over, stop the car and let her out. Every woman I know remembers the time the man she was with pulled over, stopped the car and she actually got out.

I confess I'm not much fun on road trips. This particular human failing, like most human failings, can be traced back to my childhood when I was could have been elected poster boy for car sickness, a condition that runs in my family. My parents watched me anxiously, dreading each curve and bump. Their only suggestion was that I roll down my window and hold out a Kleenex. In theory, the tissue, flapping like a white flag of surrender, was supposed to take my mind off my nausea; in practice, we were routinely stopped for littering.

While I've grown out of my car sickness, I still get cranky as a kid after I've been driving for a long time. I may not say it in so many words, but the question "Are we there yet?" is always on my mind.

This is not an inherited trait. My father loved nothing more than to get in the car and drive, the wind in his hair, his elbow out the window. On the hottest summer day, he disdained air conditioning. The idea of driving with his elbow tucked in by his side was unthinkable to him.

My father, incidentally, made all his road trips from the passenger seat. Crippled by polio, he never learned to drive. It was an indication of just how passionate he felt about the open road that he bought our first family car before anyone in our family knew how to drive. He assumed that one of my older sisters would learn. But it was my mother, then well into her forties, who was first to get her license.

She was a tentative driver at first. Later on, she invented her own unique coping strategies. I remember being stuck on a steep incline in the Laurentian Mountains. Our first car had a standard transmission, and my mother, who hadn't yet mastered the timing required to release the clutch and engage the accelerator without stalling, waved ahead the dozen cars stopped behind her. Then she calmly rolled to the bottom of the hill and tried again—successfully—on level ground.

My sisters and I were often embarrassed driving with my mother. Not my father. His support was unconditional, fanatical. And as we got further from our suburban home and from city traffic, he'd urge her to go faster. "Shoot," he'd say. "Shoot."

I realize now that my father had the right idea. "To travel hopefully is better than to arrive," Robert Louis Stevenson said. The best road trips, like the best relationships, are less about arriving at your destination and more about enjoying the journey—as well as the person next to you.

I'll try to remember that the next time my partner and I head out on the open road. If I'm not at the wheel, I'll glance over at her and say, "Shoot."

"All right, Snookums," she'll say. "Hold on to your Kleenex."

Old Confetti

In the summer of 1977 an outbreak of marital activity swept through my small circle of male friends like a flu making the rounds. In the span of three months, I must have attended a half dozen weddings. I wouldn't have guessed it at the time, but that would be as many as I would attend in the next two decades. The contagion wouldn't catch me either, something else I might not have guessed at the time.

Because back then, caught up in other people's plans and ceremonies, I wasn't as convinced as I am now that I was cut out to be a bachelor. So what if I didn't have any prospects of a relationship or a job? These were just minor obstacles. I attended each wedding with an eagerness and a curiosity that astonished and pleased me. It all felt like necessary research.

I remember very little about that summer now, except for a blur of stag parties, I Do's, tossed bouquets and scattered confetti. There's one moment, though, that still stands out and that's when my friend Wayne knelt in front of the altar to take his vows with the words HELP ME! spelled out in white adhesive tape on the soles of his shoes. A whispering campaign spread through the church pews. Those people who could see what all the fuss was about were telling those who couldn't, until everyone knew about the prank except the minister, the bride and the groom. The question everyone was asking was, "Who could have done such a thing?" The smart money was on the best man.

Obviously, the only person who would have had the nerve to do it, let alone the means and the opportunity, was the groom himself. Naturally, there were a few people at the wedding who didn't find this gag funny—the bride's family, for example—but most of us, particularly Wayne's male friends, thought it was a brilliant, daring joke. A welcome reminder that we were still, at heart, a bunch of fun-loving, carefree guys who didn't have to take this whole marriage business too seriously.

It's only recently that I realized that this juvenile prank was really the opposite of what it seemed at the time. It was an indication of just how serious Wayne and all my friends who took the plunge that summer were about marriage. Incidentally, taking the plunge is precisely the way to describe their behavior. In their early twenties, none of my friends were either emotionally or financially secure enough to be doing what they were doing, but they did it anyway.

It's in that same spirit that a mischievous, hopeful young man stayed up late the night before his wedding and diligently cut little strips of white tape into the shape of letters and attached them to the bottom of his shoes. Only someone with unshakable confidence in the rightness of what he was doing would have had the nerve to spoof it in that way. Only someone who believed absolutely that his marriage was going to last would not have been worried about jinxing it.

Today no one I know would take that kind of chance. Today the only people who seem to be expressing a similar kind of commitment to marriage are gay. The rest of us don't have to be told the statistics, we know them by heart. Half of all marriages end in divorce. The numbers may not have been as bad twenty years ago, but they couldn't have been encouraging. Any statistical study, then or now, would have told my friends that the odds would be much better for them if they decided to hold off for a few years. But they didn't and it's incredible to me now—more incredible than ever—that they managed to go through with it at all. I could update you, give you the current statistics, I could tell you that four out of these six marriages didn't last, including Wayne's, but I'm not sure what that would prove. Except that the mistakes my friends made twenty years ago were mistakes of commission rather than omission.

The other day I discovered a package of confetti in the back of my desk drawer and experienced a brief moment of amnesia. My initial reaction was: what am I doing with this? Then I remembered. I bought it the day after my girlfriend and I spent the night together for the first time.

It was a symbolic gesture, sentimental and superstitious: a way of announcing to myself that I had finally met the woman I wanted to marry. That was three years ago and although my girlfriend and I are still together, we're not married and haven't come close. After three years, most of the tiny specks of colored paper have faded and those that haven't have turned to dust. I thought about throwing the package away, but I reconsidered and—sentimental and superstitious as ever—put it back where I found it.

Which is also a symbolic gesture: keeping the confetti, but keeping it out of sight. As much as I love my girlfriend, I am still ambivalent about our relationship—at least in the sense that I have no idea where it is going. What's more telling, perhaps, is that I have no idea where it should be going.

My girlfriend feels the same way. We are both well into our thirties and we are both suffering from chronic cases of cold feet. For both of us, this relationship is our longest and most serious. But that's all it is for now. A serious relationship. Just one more in an uninterrupted string of interrupted relationships. I can't imagine anything ever feeling as right as this, but I still wonder whether I've missed my chance. If marriage was an option once, I'm not sure that it is any more.

Early on in our relationship I remember my girlfriend informing me that she was late. I replied the way most men reply to this incomplete, out-of-the-blue bit of information and said, "Late for what?"

She stared at me until I finally got the message and I said what most men say, "Oh, you mean *late.*" She had already purchased one of those early pregnancy kits but, as it turned out, she never had to use it. She got her period the next morning.

But before she did, before we knew, we spent the day being unusually polite to each other, which is another way of saying we avoided each other. I didn't say much because I didn't think it was my place to. We'd only been together for a couple of months and I was enough of a sensitive, liberated New Man to know that any decision on this matter was hers, not mine. I also had a pretty good idea what that decision would be. The next day, after the issue had been decided for us, I asked her what she would have done, just to be sure. She confirmed what I had already thought. Having a baby was out of the question. It was crazy. Not only were we unsure of how we felt about each other at that point, we were in no position to raise a child. She had other plans. So did I.

She was being sensible, of course, and I agreed with her completely. And that's what I couldn't shake then and, to some extent, still can't shake now: how sensible we were both being, how easily I agreed with her. True, there was something gnawing at me, something inside me that said: "Why the hell not? Why not go the whole nine yards? Commitment, marriage, family." But it just wasn't saying it forcefully enough. So while there was a world of options still open to us, taking the plunge no longer seemed to be one of them.

Men are often accused of waiting for the next pretty face or the next perfect pair of breasts to come around the corner, of only being interested in conjuring up some playmate of the month or supermodel to have a fling with. I wish the explanation for our restlessness was that simple.

Men can be stupid, all right, but we're not that stupid. Most of us realize that no airbrushed fantasy will ever be as complicated or comforting or as much fun as a real relationship. "There is," according to the novelist Josephine Humphreys, "much to be said for side-by-sideness. It is, after all....the attitude of marriage. All the frontal thrill in the world will yield eventually to this lateral alignment." I love being part of a couple and, frankly, it's this "side-by-sideness" I love most. This "attitude of marriage."

My problem is I'm too sensible to believe that it will endure. At the end of the twentieth century there is—for men and women both—a Catch-22 built into all our love affairs and it's that we're too smart for our own good. We know that nothing, especially love, lasts forever. We are like the characters in a Chekhov play who keep daydreaming about going to Moscow, but never do it. Why? Because they secretly suspect that Moscow is just a big town full of more gloomy Russians who won't shut up about their dead-end lives.

So what are we really saying when we invent fancy terms like "serial monogamy" to describe our love lives? We are saying that we have our contingency plans prepared, our fallback position ready. After all, if the relationship we're involved in now doesn't work out, and there are plenty of statistics to say it won't, there will be another one to look forward to and, according to the statistics, another one after that.

Like everyone else these days—from Hollywood producers to perfume manufacturers to politicians—I want some focus group, some survey or poll, which is right eighteen times out of twenty, to tell me what my options are, what I should do next, even though I know what I should do next. I should buy myself a new package of confetti. Or just take the old one out of the drawer.

DUMPED

"If you leave me, can I come too?"
—Cynthia Heimel

The One That Got Away

Her name was Melinda Levy and she was the first girl who ever kissed me. We were both in the third grade and we'd been selected—girl and boy respectively—for some trumped up class honor, the sort of thing everyone would receive sooner or later. But that was a detail and even then I knew I had a talent for ignoring important details. All I cared about was that Melinda and I were chosen first and chosen together. I was eight, but no kid. I knew what this meant: we were made for each other.

Later, during recess, I tried my best to make her acknowledge this fact while she skipped rope with her girlfriends, trying her best to ignore me. My plan was simple enough to be brilliant: I'd keep pestering her until she noticed me. Finally, just to be rid of me, she grabbed me by the shoulders and placed her lips briefly on my forehead. Her friends squealed; I ran away. There was no more smooching after that, no lengthy conversations about our relationship either—I just assumed we were a couple.

I had our future all mapped out, too. I'd bide my time, take the summer off pretending to be a cowboy or a fireman, and come back to the fourth grade mature and ready to make a commitment.

I had also decided we'd be holding hands by Christmas and that by the spring she would have kissed me somewhere closer to my mouth. When I returned to school in September, I was anxious to see her. I'd devised all kinds of scenarios for our reunion: everything from us sitting next to each other in class to me carrying her books as I walked her home.

What happened next was the one thing I hadn't anticipated: Melinda was not in class—not that first day, not that first week. The childhood grapevine was slow, but eventually I learned that the Levy family had moved to California and—talk about bad luck—they'd taken their eight-year-old daughter with them.

In retrospect, I can't help wondering if this was more than bad luck, if it was a bad omen. The kind of scene that was bound to repeat itself, invariably accompanied by a soundtrack featuring Tom Waits, in a tattoo parlor, singing, "Don't misspell her name, buddy. She's the one that got away."

In my case, a tattoo has never been necessary. Whatever else you want to say about rejection, it certainly makes an impression. I remember the names of everyone who kissed me off as well as the names of those who I was convinced would have kissed me off if I'd ever gotten up the nerve to ask them out. In addition to Melinda, there was Susan and Suzy and Janet and Sharon and Debbie and Dorothy and Naomi and another Janet and another Suzy. And, it occurs to me, I'm still not finished listing the girls in elementary school.

I read a novel recently in which the hero, after being dumped by his current girlfriend, decides to review his "top five most memorable split-ups." An obsessive type, he also decides to look the women up to see if they can tell him where he went wrong, including the twelve year old who abruptly and without explanation ended their six hour relationship— spread out over three evenings—for a cooler guy. What the hero discovers on his preposterous sentimental journey is illuminating but not surprising. His most recent romantic foul-up is just a scrambled version of all his previous ones.

Which is why dwelling on the past is a risky business and why dwelling on lost loves—no matter how innocent or fleeting—is even riskier. Of course, we do it anyway.

We are looking for some clue, I suppose, that will reveal to us how we ended up where we are—with the person we're with or not with the person we'd like to be with. Maybe what we're really looking for is some secret which, once uncovered, will clear everything up. What we are likely to find is the opposite. Like children playing peekaboo, the only secret is the one we seem to be concealing from ourselves. Every mistake we make we've made before.

Maybe that's why I can't help thinking my reminiscence about Melinda Levy isn't a story about bad timing as much as it is a story about missed opportunities. As unseemly as it is these days to blame my inner child for how I turned out, I have to face facts: the kid acted like a wimp. It may have been the first time, but it wouldn't be the last.

A few years later, in high school, when I was set up on a roller skating date with Gail Herscovici, a cute blonde who, amazingly enough, seemed to like me, I stood her up because I couldn't roller skate and didn't want to look foolish. More bad luck, I told myself with a straight face. Several years after that, working at a summer job, I did everything I could to get Madeleine Macmillan, one of my coworkers, to like me. Everything, that is, except asking her out. I was waiting for just the right moment and when it finally came, at the end of the summer, it coincided with a realization that Madeleine had been getting a lift home every night in another coworker's Trans-Am and that they seemed to be sitting extremely close to each other. Bad timing, I told myself, again with a straight face.

Mavis Gallant was right: "People do not remember what they have done, but only what was done to them." I know why too. Because going over all the missed and messed up opportunities usually turns out to be a little too educational.

It's a safe bet, for instance, that the eight year old who pestered little girls in the playground and received an unexpected kiss on the forehead for his trouble would still be pestering women some thirty years later. The same eight year old who couldn't distinguish between infatuation and the real thing, who assumed, from watching too many old movies, that two people really could be made for each other would never let go of that preposterous notion. And so, much later when he fell in love, for what may have been the first time, with a woman who kept insisting that she couldn't love him in return, that would be just one more important detail he would decide to ignore.

He would persist and pester her until she finally fell in love with him. And then when, just as unexpectedly, her feelings changed, he would never see it coming. Like Melinda Levy moving to California, it would be the one thing—the only thing—he never anticipated.

Larry Fortensky, C'est Moi

In a famous scene near the end of the gladiator epic, *Spartacus,* the Roman commander, played with sinister glee by Laurence Olivier, stands in front of thousands of captured rebels gathered on a hillside and announces that if they will just hand over their leader, their lives will be spared. As Kirk Douglas, who plays the title role, is about to reveal his identity, one of his men stands and shouts, "I am Spartacus." Then another does the same. Then another. Until all the rebels are on their feet shouting, "I am Spartacus." Kirk Douglas's eyes well up and you know exactly what he's thinking: he couldn't be prouder of these guys in togas if they were his own sons. The next day everyone, including Douglas, is crucified by the side of the road.

Believe it or not, this qualifies as a happy ending for most guys. Despite our competitive natures, it's a male fantasy to think that when the chips are down we can count on each other in a way that we can't always count on women. Why do you think little boys all want to grow up to be policemen and firemen? Why do you think there are still organizations with secret handshakes and funny hats and no girls allowed? From Sydney Carton in *A Tale of Two Cities* to David Hasselhoff in *Baywatch,* our stories are full of stirring examples of sacrifice, of one guy laying down his life or his suntan lotion for another.

The other side of the story, the one that is usually overlooked, is that nothing undermines a man's sense of obligation to his fellow man faster than a woman with other plans. Just imagine if instead of Laurence Olivier standing on the hill, there had been a woman asking, "Who left the toilet seat up?" You know what would have happened: everyone would have been pointing at Kirk Douglas and shouting, "Spartacus did it."

This is our secret shame: our willingness to turn on each other just to impress a woman and get on her good side. We are all potential traitors—fifth columnists at heart, waiting for our chance to blow the whistle. In Garrison Keillor's *The Book of Guys*, there is a disturbing but candid confession. "For more than thirty years, I have been nudging women and pointing out dopey men to them," Keillor writes, "so that women would know that I am no bozo."

What man hasn't done the same thing? We've all betrayed our own gender just so we could set ourselves apart from some guy who was behaving like a jerk.

"You know why So-And-So sleeps around," we'll say to the woman we're with, reassuring her as much about our willingness to pass judgement on another guy as our fidelity, "it's because he's overcompensating. He's insecure about his sexuality." They will nod, having heard us echo what they already believed to be true, and we will have made our point, which is that we are nothing like that. They can trust us: we are barely jerks at all.

There is a complacency that grows like mold on anyone who is happily paired off and that is impossible to recognize when you are the one who is happily paired off. It's only later that you wonder how you didn't see it all along. It's only in retrospect that it is embarrassing to describe. Now that my girlfriend and I have broken up or, more accurately, now that she has dumped me, I realize how cavalier I have often been in poking fun at other relationships and, in particular, at the behavior of other men in those relationships. Now, I'm also embarrassed to admit, my attitude has changed. There is a Brotherhood of the Dumped. I know because I'm part of it. I know because lately I find myself worrying far more than I ever thought possible about the sad fate of Larry Fortensky.

In 1991, Elizabeth Taylor said "I do" for the eighth time (that's counting Richard Burton twice) to a man twenty years her junior. There was no need to make up jokes. The facts were silly enough all by themselves: the movie star and this Larry guy, who *People* magazine dubbed "a burly, curly construction worker," fell in love at the Betty Ford Clinic and were married at Michael Jackson's Neverland ranch where a sky diver—hoping, perhaps, to put in an early bid to be husband number nine—crashed the ceremony, missing the altar by twenty feet.

A few years later, when Liz announced that she and Larry were separating because they each needed their own space, no one even pretended to be surprised. Instead, the overwhelming reaction was what had taken so long? When the inevitable happened and the separation turned into yet another divorce, the media and the public would continue to fret about poor Liz—about her hip replacements, her fluctuating weight, her addiction problems, her failed business ventures, her romantic judgement.

But no one gave Larry Fortensky a second thought. He'd already managed to get through a very public marriage and divorce to one of the most famous women in the world without ever saying a word and now he would disappear completely. *People* magazine, breaking the news of the separation, used the headline: "FAREWELL FORTENSKY." They might as well have called the article GOOD RIDDANCE or HASTA LA VISTA, LARRY. No one even considered feeling sorry for the guy.

Except me. That's the thing about being dumped: you find yourself empathizing with the most unlikely people. Bozos, in other words. Does misery love company? Does it ever.

I visited a friend recently who was in the middle of getting a divorce from her husband of ten years. Two of her female friends were already at her house, helping her pack her soon-to-be-ex's clothing and other belongings into boxes and moving all his stuff to the basement where it would be stored until he showed up to claim it. The job was a tedious one and, as the day wore on, there was a lot of badmouthing of men in general from the three women, who had five divorces among them, and a lot of badmouthing of my friend's husband, in particular, whom everyone referred to as Creepface.

For my part, I helped carry the boxes downstairs, but I didn't feel good about participating in what was turning into a ritual exorcism. My ambivalence surprised me. I knew Creepface and had never thought of him as a kindred spirit. Like a lot of other people, I wondered what my friend had seen in him in the first place and was convinced that she was well rid of him. So what exactly was bothering me?

I couldn't put my finger on it until I saw an old refrigerator pushed into a dark corner of the basement. It was unplugged and it had two beer spigots screwed into the front door. I asked my friend what it was. "That's his," she said and opened the door to show me how the spigots were attached to long tubes which led to a large plastic tank in the middle of the otherwise gutted, shelfless appliance. "He built it for parties. His pride and joy." All three women laughed simultaneously, then shook their heads and went back upstairs to continue packing.

I remained in the basement and, for the first time ever, felt a twinge of sympathy for Creepface, felt a connection to him, thinking about all the effort he must have put into this contraption, and all the pride he must have taken in showing it to his buddies.

Sure, it was silly, an enormous waste of time and energy—time and energy he might have been investing in his relationship—but it was also ingenious in that way that only completely preposterous things are. And here it was: discarded, an object of ridicule, like all men whose best laid plans don't work out—whether we're leading a futile rebellion against ancient Rome or just hoping the woman we love will love us forever.

"Spectacular dumbness is a guy type of gift," Garrison Keillor also said. "We are good at great schemes and failed behavior." Examining the refrigerator that had been

transformed into a homemade keg, I held on for a moment—
a moment I knew would pass—to the vague hope that I would
have, along with all my misery-loves-company compatriots on
that Roman hillside, stood up and said, "Yeah, sure, I'm
Spartacus, too. Count me in." At the very least, I knew I could
say with conviction and a certain amount of embarrassment,
"I am Creepface." As for Elizabeth Taylor's vanished and
unlamented ex: Larry Fortensky, *c'est moi*.

Tears of a Clown

I can't remember anyone ever telling me when I was growing up that I wasn't supposed to hit a girl, but it was still something I always knew. I certainly knew it when I punched Elaine Eichenbaum in the mouth. She sat one desk behind me in the second grade, where it seemed to me that her purpose in life was to make my life miserable.

In retrospect, her pestering and teasing was probably a sign that she liked me, but, then as now, I tend to overlook the obvious. All I remember is the dread I felt at the end of the school day. That's when each student was required to put his or her chair up on the desk. Because I was one of the smallest kids in class, it was often a struggle for me to lift my chair over my head. Elaine would wait for this moment and then routinely call attention to it, pointing at me and teasing me in front of my classmates.

I put up with the teasing for a long time until one day walking home from school she called me a wimp or whatever the elementary school equivalent of wimp was at the time and I hit her as hard as I could. Her lip began to bleed and she ran home crying. Even though I knew she had it coming and even though she never teased me again, I also knew I'd acted improperly—that I'd breached some unwritten code.

That was the only time I ever hit a girl and the only time I ever considered it until a little while ago. This time the girl in question was my ex and though we'd been apart for several months, we'd worked out a plan to try to remain friends.

We broke up around the time of the Quebec referendum and so we liked to refer to our plan as our own variation on sovereignty-association. This meant we still went out to movies and dinner together, we were just no longer a couple, in the official sense. On more than one occasion I remember reading or watching TV while she undressed for bed, lay down beside me and fell asleep. Other than the fact that I went home to my own bed at the end of the evening, it was hard sometimes to figure out what had changed.

I also remember thinking that our experiment in a new kind of partnership might have broader implications for the entire Canadian confederation. Naturally, there were glitches and, as with any effort to legislate human behavior, rules and conditions were required. I came up with two. First, if she ever wanted to have sex with me, you know, for old times' sake, she would just let me know. Second, if she ever started seeing someone else she would also let me know.

This may come as a shock to some people, particularly here in the province of Quebec, but sovereignty-association isn't going to work. Go figure. The obvious problem: one side will inevitably want a lot more sovereignty, the other side a lot more association.

I called my ex one day after not speaking to her for a couple of weeks and as soon as I heard the slight tremor of hesitation in her voice, followed by the words, "I have something to tell you," I knew what it was. I was so sure, in fact, that when I didn't respond and she began to repeat that she had something to tell me, I interrupted and said, "Who is he?"

From there, our conversation consisted of me pressuring her to see me one more time, and her insisting that she didn't think talking about this now would do either of us any good.

"Have you slept with him?" I finally asked. It took all my effort to use the word "slept."

"Yes," she said.

Now I had something real to imagine and something real to feel. My heart tightened. I felt dizzy and disoriented and, most of all, I felt foolish. Something like this was bound to happen. Who did we think we were kidding? Stay friends—it's never been done. At least not when one person still loves the other person. She was right, too: talking about it wouldn't do either of us any good.

"I have to talk to you," I said anyway.

"I told you it's not a good idea."

"I don't care. I'm coming over. You don't have to let me in if you don't want to, but I'm coming anyway," I said and hung up on her. It was bad enough that she had decided to start seeing someone else, I wasn't going to let her decide how I should handle the situation, even if she was right. Especially if she was right.

The drive into town to her apartment usually takes thirty minutes. I did it in half that. All the while I felt an unfamiliar rage building inside me and I kept thinking the same thing: that she had betrayed me and that I wanted nothing more than to hurt her. Of course, she hadn't done any such thing. We were no longer a couple. We were both entitled to see whomever we wanted. I knew that then as well as I know it now, it was just easier then to pretend that I didn't.

When I arrived at her apartment, she buzzed me up, though I'm not so sure she would have if her building had had an intercom and she had been able to hear the anger in my voice or if she had been able to see me. There are lots of reasons why too many men beat their lovers or wives and I was getting a close-up look at one of them. The one that is less about a need for control or vengeance and more about the need to deny weakness and vulnerability.

I apologize if this sounds like an excuse, but I am an overeducated, overly polite man who was raised in the suburbs. In most respects, I have lived a sheltered, tame life and the only thing I know about my own potential for violence I was learning that afternoon.

Some twenty years ago when my mother died, I put my fist through my bedroom wall. I remember being astonished when the plaster crumbled and yielded. The act was automatic, a logical response to an unbearable situation. But this time, as I walked up the four flights of stairs to my ex's apartment, faced with another unbearable situation, I was aware that my fists were clenched. I knew exactly what I was doing, I knew it was wrong, but I intended to do it anyway. Not only that, I found the idea of doing it exhilarating. Evil is a loaded word, impossible to define, but I think I was learning something about evil that afternoon, too .

Never mind that I was acting mostly out of anguish and regret. Never mind that I was allowing my disappointment to be fueled by jealousy and turned into rage and that the rage was welcome. Never mind that I knew none of it would last. All that mattered is that I wanted it to last.

But by the time I saw my ex standing in her doorway, leaning forlornly against the wall, my fists were already unclenched. I took a deep breath and probably looked pretty forlorn myself. We hugged briefly and clumsily and we spent the next two hours talking. Occasionally, I raised my voice and angrily paced around her apartment, but that was all. With the rage gone, though, my jealousy had nothing to conceal itself behind. It was naked and it was pitiful.

I drifted through her apartment looking for signs of the other man. I noticed an unfamiliar magazine on the night table next to what used to be my side of the bed. There was an unfamiliar toothbrush in the bathroom. I also looked for signs that I had been displaced once and for all and found those too. The photograph of me that had been on the bulletin board in her office was gone. The throw rug on which we had made love and on which I had once left a stain in what I liked to imagine was the shape of a tiny heart and which I jokingly thought of as our only child, was discreetly turned over. Some joke.

We hugged again when I left. She cried and, as was usually the case, I ended up comforting her. I reserved my crying for later, doing it the way a man is supposed to, stopped at a traffic light, alone in my car, with Smokey Robinson, at full volume, singing "Tears of a Clown" on the radio. Somewhere in the city there's an elderly woman in a two-toned Toyota Cressida who can vouch for me.

There's a scene in Marcel Proust's *Swann in Love* in which the title character discovers that his mistress Odette has been unfaithful to him and he suddenly, unexpectedly, bursts into sobs. Self-conscious characters are the rule rather than the exception in Proust and so Swann also has the presence of mind to stop for a moment, chuckle and say to himself, "This is delightful. I am becoming a neurasthenic."

All right, I thought, pulling the car over to the side of the road, if I can't be an accomplished jealous lunatic, I can at least be a neurasthenic. But I knew that career would be short-lived too. That's the problem with putting on an act, even one you want to believe. When it's over you have to go back to being who you were before. Which is, it occurs to me now, what I'd been trying to avoid all along.

Closure, Anyone?

Although I'm prepared to admit that the guy who said "it's better to have loved and lost then never to have loved at all" was probably right, I'm not sure he had to be so damn smug about it. Those of us who are trying to cope with being dumped need more than platitudes, we need a psychological game plan. Towards that end, I've developed two basic survival strategies for guys who've had their hearts broken. The first one is to take it like a man. This will require you to move beyond your own bitterness and disappointment and tell the person who just broke your heart that you wish her well.

However, if you do this, be prepared: your ex will likely respond by saying that she hopes the two of you can remain friends. Worse still, she could say that she will always love you, even though she's not in love with you any more. Remember, in both cases, it's bad form to gag or retch or otherwise threaten to throw up. You should also refrain from crying like a baby, whining, wheedling, begging and cajoling the other person to take you back. The most you can do is make some joke, preferably a small and feeble one, about how you will even miss the way she hogs the blankets at night.

This strategy, also known as the high road, has advantages and disadvantages. On the plus side, after you've left her apartment for the last time, only you will know how much you really feel like throwing up. On the negative side, the chance of breakup sex is remote.

The second strategy, otherwise known as the low road, primarily consists of whining, wheedling, begging and cajoling the other person to take you back. And, yes, throwing up. It goes without saying that this strategy has some obvious weaknesses. On the plus side, though, there is a slightly better chance of breakup sex.

But, remember, whichever method you choose, the most important thing is never to use both at the same time. A lesson I learned the hard way. One moment, there I was, urbane as Noel Coward, chatting amiably with my ex about the weather or some mutual acquaintance, then a moment later I was falling apart and carrying on about how much I missed her. Needless to say, this kind of behavior tends to be counterproductive. Displaying a dual personality may also bring you the kind of unsolicited advice Dr. Jekyl and Mr. Hyde were always getting. "You might want to think about talking to someone. You know, someone objective," is the way my ex put it to me on more than one occasion.

Frankly, I don't see the point. I know what a shrink will tell me. A shrink will tell me that I need closure and a shrink will be right. But, as advice goes, this falls, like most psychological advice, into the so-what-else-is-new category. Everyone needs closure; everyone also needs free cable and more oral sex. Needing it is not the point; our inability to obtain it is.

A competent therapist will explain, for example, that the first thing you have to realize about closure is that you're on your own. You can't rely on anyone else to give it to you. Unfortunately, this runs counter to my own solution to the problem, which has been to call my ex up every other week and ask her what she thinks I should do next to get over her. True, she hasn't had any helpful suggestions yet, but, as it happens, I'm in no rush.

A competent therapist may also recommend the following two-part technique for achieving closure. First, write a comprehensive goodbye letter and put everything you have to say about your failed relationship into it. Second, do not, under any circumstances, mail this letter. The good news is that I wrote the letter. You can probably guess the bad news.

In strictly psychological terms, closure can best be defined as the necessary process of accepting a situation or set of circumstances you are not yet ready to accept. In layman's terms—this layman anyway—closure sucks.

I don't need a shrink to tell me that the one thing I have to do to recover from being dumped is put a reasonable time frame on my recovery period. What I need is someone to tell me what is reasonable. In the meantime, I've decided that if I'm not over my ex by the time Canada resolves its constitutional crisis I'll move on whether I'm ready to or not.

I guess all I'm trying to say is that even though closure may be fine for some people, it's just not working out for me. Luckily, I've come up with an alternative. The British psychiatrist John Bowlby says that since the standard response to the loss of a loved one is the urge to recover them, it follows that this urge is an automatic one, built into human nature like a hunger or thirst and that it "will come into action in response to any and every loss....without discriminating between those that are retrievable and those that are not." Bowlby calls this "the attachment theory."

Leave it to a psychiatrist to make this sound like a bad thing. As far as I'm concerned, "the attachment theory" is right up there with denial as just about the most fun you can have coping with a completely unacceptable reality.

Personally, I prefer British writer Catherine Heath's solution. In her novel *Behaving Badly,* she tells the story of Bridget Mayor, a middle-aged suburban housewife whose husband decides to leave her for a younger woman. For five years, Bridget behaves the way she is expected to. She takes up hobbies, registers for courses, gets on with her life. One day, though, it suddenly occurs to her that the life she is living is not one she likes or wants very much and she moves back in with her husband and his new wife.

She is not resentful or jealous—as a matter of fact, she gets along quite well with her husband's new wife—she is simply unwilling to accept the reality someone else has decided to impose on her. By the end, Bridget has not only become the hero of the novel, she has become my hero. She is an important test case, too—proof that "the attachment theory" can be much more than a theory, it can be a way of life.

The question raised by *Behaving Badly* is not whether this is a healthy thing for Bridget to be doing. Of course it isn't. Or whether it will resolve anything. It doesn't. Or whether it will make it easier for her to get on with her life. It won't. The real question is does she have a point? The answer to that is: you bet she does.

Masturbation: A Love Story

It first occurred to me I might be taking myself for granted when I saw Gloria Steinem on television a couple of years ago staring meaningfully and lovingly at her own reflection in the mirror. According to her memoir, *Revolution from Within: A Book of Self-Esteem,* Ms. Steinem, who apparently didn't have any self-esteem for a long time, though no one would have guessed it, and who now seems to be lousy with the stuff, has learned an old but reliable lesson: if you can't love yourself first, you'll never be able to love anyone else.

Which is why I've started leaving notes around the house for myself. Nothing too forward. I don't want to scare myself off or start talking commitment just yet. Frankly, I'm not sure I'm ready. Anyway, it's best, at the start of any relationship, to give yourself—or, in this case, myself—some space. No one—also, in this case, me—likes to be rushed or pressured. It's worth remembering that these are the nineties and sexual harassment is no longer a joking matter. The lessons of Pee Wee Herman and Michael Jackson—both vilified for touching themselves—haven't been lost on me either: nothing good can come from taking unfair advantage of yourself. So my motto thus far has been: nice and easy does it.

I've also decided to keep things casual for now. The notes I leave for myself—usually on my pillow or beside my toothbrush—are open-ended and invariably say something like:

If you're not doing anything later, maybe we can go for a walk or catch a movie?!?

Love, Me.

To demonstrate just how new all this is for me, I even worried initially about how to address myself. Was it too forward, for example, to use the word "love"? Was I undermining all my efforts to take things slow? In the end, though, I chose the word "love" because it would have seemed absurd, after everything I've been through with myself, to end with, Your Best Pal. Or, With Fondest Wishes, You Know Who. Or even, Yours Truly, Yours Truly.

But despite these awkward moments which, after all, occur in every relationship, I am pleased to report that everything seems to be progressing fine. Without having to kiss and tell, I think I can safely say: so far, so good. I suppose I shouldn't be surprised. After all, I'm a nice enough guy. Given the right circumstances, I can be charming and witty. I'm respectful and patient, a good listener, a good dancer, a snappy dresser.

Still, I won't lie—it hasn't always been easy. In the past, I haven't always given myself a chance to get in the mood, let alone say, "No, not tonight, honey. My wrist hurts."

Let's face it, when it comes to dating myself, I've become accustomed to going, as we used to say when we were kids, all the way. That's the way it has been ever since I was twelve.

But what I am beginning to understand now is that I've never really shown myself the proper respect, the kind of respect I would routinely show anyone else I was interested in. It's pretty much been slam bam, thank you, fella. This is an unhappy fact about my past relationship with myself that I need to accept, embrace even, before I can move on.

Fortunately, what I've learned recently is that self-love can indeed be loving. More to the point, self-abuse doesn't have to be abusive. Lately, I've gotten into the habit of calling myself by a pet name, which I've promised myself I'd keep a secret. Occasionally, I'll send myself flowers or a heart-shaped balloon. I also know how I feel about take-out Chinese food so, on special occasions, I'll spring for dinner number two for one. I've been considerate and kind—the perfect gentleman.

Maybe too much of a gentleman. Just the other night for example, I was at home, alone, glancing at the *Victoria Secret* catalogue that had come in the mail in the morning and I began feeling a little, well, romantic. Just as I got to the lingerie pages, though, I could hear a voice in the back of my head saying, "That's what you're going to wear?"

And while it's true that I could have put on a new bathrobe instead of one that was fraying at the sleeves, and maybe one of my socks had a hole in it—though I doubt it—I was still hurt. After everything I'd been through recently to make myself feel more appreciated, here I was playing hard to get.

The truth was undeniable: I didn't care about myself as much as I thought I did and after an exchange of some angry words, I got dressed and stormed out of the house. Every relationship is unequal. There is always the pursued, on the one hand, and, on the other hand, the pursuer. But still there were things said that night which I wasn't sure I'd ever be able to take back.

And so for days, I've barely talked to myself. I've started to wonder if I really know myself at all. I'm worried and I'm not ashamed to admit it. Which is why I have turned to Ms. Steinem's book again for inspiration and have taken comfort in another passage about her ongoing struggle to love herself. It's reassuring to find out that even now the New Gloria and Old Gloria aren't always on the best terms. Near the end of the book, Ms. Steinem, addressing herself in the third person, admits:

"I used to feel impatient with her: Why was she wasting time? ...Why wasn't she wiser, more productive, happier? But lately, I've begun to feel a tenderness, a welling of tears in the back of my throat, when I see her. I think: She's doing the best she can.... Sometimes, I wish I could go back and put my arms around her."

Me too. More than anything else, I want to make up with myself. I've decided to tell myself I'm sorry for everything. From now on, I'm going to be open and honest. From now on, I can promise myself this much—one hand will always know what the other one is doing.

Bachelorhood

Winston Churchill defined success as the ability to "go from failure to failure with no loss of enthusiasm." But then, all Churchill had to worry about was losing World War II. He didn't have his friends trying to fix him up, calling him unexpectedly to say, "Winnie, we know someone who would be just perfect for you. We told her all about you and she thought your "fight them on the beaches" speech was really cute. Adorable, even. Adorable, that's exactly how she put it. So what do you say?"

I don't mean to imply by this that friends are not a great source of comfort, because they are, particularly after a long relationship ends. Indeed, that's when they are most indispensable. Who else will tell you that the woman you loved so completely and unreservedly wasn't right for you in the first place? Your friends, that's who.

"Didn't you ever notice how shifty her eyes were?" they'll say. "Honestly, we don't know how you put up with her as long as you did."

They'll also tell you that they saw this coming all along, but kept this relatively crucial information to themselves. "We didn't want to hurt you," they'll explain, free to offer their advice retroactively, now that you have been hurt.

But even more indispensable than the moral support friends provide is their philosophical perspective. Who else will tell you that life goes on and that time heals all wounds? Only your friends. It's a good thing too, since if anyone else had the nerve to make such inane, clichéd and, worst of all, accurate remarks when you are in so much distress, you'd probably never talk to them again.

But your friends only want what's best for you and, after hearing you moan and complain for months about how miserable you are, they've come to the conclusion that what's best for you is to be fixed up with someone new and they know just the person. There are usually two reasons they come to this conclusion: first, because they genuinely care about you. Second, because they have problems of their own and they'd like to get back to them, if you don't mind.

Hell is not other people, as Jean Paul Sartre said. Hell is other people trying to fix you up with other people. Usually, that means the friend of a friend of a guy who was the cousin of another guy who sells wholesale jewelry out of his house and it turns out you met her once but you probably don't remember because you were drinking back then and it was just before her operation so, technically speaking, she was still a man at the time.

Which makes me believe that not quite as much thought goes into these perfect matches as you are initially led to believe. Most of the time, they are just a shot in the dark. If your friends are like mine, they won't always coordinate their efforts either. At a dinner party not long ago I ended up with three dates. This only made going home alone three times more depressing.

I am approaching that stage of life when I should be looking forward to the mid-life crisis all the experts on male psychology have been promising me for years, the kind that makes men wear their hair in a ponytail, buy flashy sportscars and run off with women half their age. Instead, I am spending this precious time at dinner parties, making small talk with friends of friends who are probably as embarrassed as I am to be out and at loose ends.

What couples take for granted—what I take for granted when I am part of a couple—is how hard it is to get to know someone from scratch. So while it's true that there are few things as irritating as the predictable habits of someone you love, it's also true that there's a shorthand that exists between people in relationships that makes the dumbest jokes funny and the most unremarkable moments poignant and memorable.

For men, even harder than the prospect of getting to know someone new is the prospect of allowing yourself to be known all over again. It's a minefield out there and you have to be aware of everything you do and say. Especially what you say.

Fixed up with a blind date recently, I spent most of the evening on a roll, criticizing a well-known, overrated novelist only to find out that the person I was with loved every book he had ever written. What's more, she was spearheading a campaign to see that he was nominated for the Nobel Prize for literature. She may have also said that she was currently looking into the possibility that this man was her long-lost biological father, but I can't be sure because by that point I wasn't really listening. I was babbling incoherently instead, trying my best to take back everything I had said: "You see, when I say his novels are pretentious crap, I mean that in the best sense."

I also have to be concerned that someone who doesn't really know me may misinterpret my charming, self-deprecating sense of humor as an indication that I have a frighteningly low opinion of myself. So I do my best to treat these dates as if they were job interviews. I try to be positive and upbeat, a regular Dale Carnegie, but I'm afraid there is a limit to how long I can keep up the act.

Like me, the poet Philip Larkin was one of those guys who wasn't always a lot of fun on a date. His biography recounts the time when Larkin, then twenty-two, lapsed into a stony silence in the middle of dinner. The woman he was with wondered if she had said something to offend him. "No," he replied, "I have just thought what it would be like to be old and have no one to look after you."

Not surprisingly, Larkin spent the rest of his life not dating much, writing poems about loneliness and disappointment instead, and amassing an impressive collection of smutty magazines. He became the prototypical crabby old bachelor.

Which is one alternative to allowing yourself to be fixed up. I have been a bachelor intermittently in the past and I am a bachelor again and I can't say I'm looking forward to a future spent putting my back issues of *Playboy* and *Penthouse* in chronological order.

Even so, I have to admit that lately I find myself staring at women—their breasts, in particular—much more than I ever used to. I don't know what it is, but they seem to be everywhere and bigger than ever. Perhaps it's the bachelor's lot to focus on externals—to make the most of his hard-earned right to be superficial. Or maybe, when it comes to breasts, I just can't get the thought out of my head that I, too, used to have access to those. Either way, I can't help worrying about turning into some kind of small-time Hugh Hefner. All I'm missing are the slippers and the silk pajamas.

Another sign that I am slipping comfortably back into bachelorhood is that I now seem to be demonstrating an uncanny ability to make my friends uncomfortable. Someone will complain about their wife or girlfriend and I'll let out a loud sigh. The kind of sigh that is easily interpreted as meaning, "At least you have someone to complain about." Which may be another reason why my friends keep trying to fix me up.

The Italian novelist and lifelong bachelor Cesar Pavase once wrote about himself in a letter: "He wants to be alone—and he is alone—but he wants to be alone in a circle of friends aware of his loneliness." Poor Cesar, he was probably always being introduced to some *amiche* of some *amiche* who lives in Venice and has a great personality. It's a vicious circle, all right.

Still, I am tempted to say that there are worse things than being a bachelor, except that one scientific study after another keeps proving me wrong. The polls are in, the surveys completed. You must have heard, as I have, that statistically speaking, there is no more unhealthy or unhappy creature on the face of the earth than a single man. Unless it's a married woman. There's just one logical solution to this dilemma: if I'm going to get married it will have to be to someone who's already married. After all, there's no reason for both of us to be unhappy.

Partygoing

I was fourteen when I stopped being popular. It happened suddenly, without explanation or warning, and I'd rather not talk about it right now, if you don't mind. There was, however, one unexpected advantage to no longer being part of the in-crowd—at least I stopped being invited to parties.

No more hiding behind sofas, waiting to jump out and shout "Surprise!" at people who looked more frightened than happy. No more dressing up in ridiculous outfits for Halloween either.

Costume parties are, by definition, embarrassing. After the initial recognition that you are, indeed, dressed like a circus clown, which lasts about thirty seconds, you are doomed to spend the next five hours discussing deficit reduction and the crisis in the Middle East wearing a big red rubber nose and shoes several sizes too big for you.

Even worse is when no one can figure out who or what you are supposed to be. I remember wearing a plumed hat, tights, a ruffled shirt and an eye patch to one Halloween party. I was also carrying a sword and a shopping bag. I waited patiently until someone asked me to identify myself. When my opportunity finally came, I said, "I am the Count of Monty Hall."

I had to explain the costume and the joke, as I probably do now. "Remember there was this game show, *Let's Make a Deal*," I said. "People dressed up and carried shopping bags in case the host, Monty Hall, asked them to produce some unusual item. Remember Alexandre Dumas's classic novel, *The Count of Monte Cristo*? Now do you get it? Count of Monty Hall?"

"I'm a pirate," I told the next person even before she asked me who I was.

"Sure, I knew that," she said, "but what's with the shopping bag?"

Still, no matter how much I complain about parties, no matter how well I can predict all the things that can and do go wrong, it's not really parties I dislike, it's being invited to them. I've just never been selective enough. I go wherever and whenever I'm asked. I'm always the last to leave.

Why? Because I'm afraid of missing something. That one enchanted moment people will be talking about for years to come: an enlightening exchange of repartee, an impromptu game of strip poker, hot hor d'oeuvres—I've never been to a party so bad it couldn't be redeemed by tiny egg rolls—or a stranger's glance across a crowded room. When you are newly single you are always being invited to parties you would never dream of going to if you were in a relationship. It's an unassailable rule of partygoing: the more desperate you are to meet someone the odder the people at the party will be.

Nevertheless, you go because there is the vague promise that there will be someone there you don't want to risk missing. You go for the same reason you buy lottery tickets. Just because your numbers haven't come up yet doesn't mean they never will. You're probably due. We probably all are.

Take a moment, now, and remember every New Year's Eve party you ever attended and then tell me I'm wrong:

11:59 p.m.: You're forced to watch Dick Clark.

12:00 a.m.: You kiss dozens of strangers, on the mouth.

12:01 a.m.: Your host plays "Celebration" by Kool and the Gang.

12:02 a.m.
–5:00 a.m.: You wonder why, if you are, after all, another year closer to death, you are spending the time you have left kissing strangers, on the mouth, and listening to Kool and the Gang.

I've had some of the most traumatic experiences of my life at parties—and that's not even counting New Year's Eve. For example, there's the time I wet my pants celebrating a friend's seventh birthday. I was seven myself and too shy to ask where the bathroom was. The urine stain spread down the front of my beige corduroys like the map of South America and that's not even the worst part. The worst part was that somehow I convinced myself no one had noticed. I stayed until the end.

I guess I'm just a party animal. Too bad the animal has to be a sheep. Elbow to elbow in a room full of fascinating, glittering strangers I have a tendency to glom onto the one person I know, even if I only know that person remotely, even if that person is about as interesting as flat beer, even if I despise that person intensely. Anything is better than mingling.

Next to root canal, visits to the proctologist and conversations that begin with the words, "we have to talk," mingling is one of my least favorite human activities. I'm not very good at it either. I have the same bad habit a lot of people do: I tend to look around the room when I am talking to someone in the hope of spotting someone else more interesting. Of course, I don't know why I bother, because even if I do see someone more interesting I still haven't mastered the enormous skill required to extricate myself from a boring person. Instead, I just end up waiting until the eyes of the person I am talking to start to wander.

All of this may explain why when the city of Montreal decided a few years ago to commemorate its 350th birthday with an extended party, I wasn't sure whether to jump up and down for joy or worry. Over the course of one winter the novelist Henry James accepted one hundred and seven dinner invitations, which was probably some kind of record—at least until Montreal's city officials decided to make their birthday bash last four months long. Every day a list of events in the official "Montreal: Let's Celebrate" calendar were printed in the newspaper and announced on the radio. Every day the list seemed to get longer and more elaborate. Didn't anyone worry about the effect that a one hundred and twenty day celebration would have on the population? Were studies done? Did anyone consider the long term side-effects of all that accumulated *joie de vivre*.

Obviously not. The worst thing about partygoing—the pressure to enjoy yourself no matter what—was being spread out over an entire summer and, like a lot of people, I was paralyzed by the sheer weight of all that forced hoopla. After a while, I couldn't bring myself to do anything except hole up in my room, pacing back and forth, marking off the activities I might attend and participate in, only to end up skipping them all. That's right, I became the one thing I'd spent my whole life desperately trying not to be—a party pooper.

Thinking back, I know where I went wrong. I attended the lavish, crowded opening night parade with too much enthusiasm, too much anticipation. I remember, as I eagerly waited for the procession down Montreal's main street, Boulevard Saint-Laurent, to commence, I saw through the crowd of some two hundred and fifty thousand spectators an attractive young woman walking toward me. This, I thought, focusing on the beaming, joyful smile on her face, is what it's all about: simple, spontaneous pleasure. But then when she came closer I also saw that she had a live rat resting, jaunty as a party hat, on top of her head. I confess that after that the parade seemed humdrum. Everything after that was, well, kind of anticlimactic.

Part of me admires that woman—her sense of *joie de vivre*, her single-minded determination to be the life of the party, her idiosyncratic choice of headgear. Then again, part of me worries about the lengths to which we will go to have a good time and the toll it takes on all of us.

As the woman walked past me and as I watched the rat's tail twitch, I tried frantically to get her attention—the way you try to get someone's attention who's driving the wrong way down a one-way street. I wanted to tell her that maybe, just maybe, she was having too much fun.

Which is the real problem I have with partygoing. There always seems to be someone having a better time than me.

HERE WE GO AGAIN

"It's not one thing after another, it's the same damn thing over and over again."

—Edna St. Vincent Millay

The Dating Game

Even as a teenager I suspected there was something paradoxical about this whole dating business. The only reason I was doing it, after all, was so I'd never have to do it again. In particular, so I'd never have to make that voice-breaking, heart-stopping telephone call to some girl I was interested in so I could, after far too much excruciating small talk, ask her the following question:

"If you're not doing, you know, anything, Saturday night, I thought, ah, maybe, assuming you're not busy, we could, um, you know, well, what's it called, go out, I don't know, somewhere, wherever, I mean if that's okay with you?"

I remember times when I was so incapable of getting anywhere near the point, when my sentences were so convoluted, that I know I was being rejected just on the basis of syntax. My solution to this problem was to scribble a few of my thoughts down on paper before I picked up the phone. Anyway, it started as just a few notes.

Before long, though, the notes became extensive. Typed. Paginated. Eventually, I was doing several drafts, including an outline, index and table of contents. I left nothing to chance. I'd even write down, "Hello" or "Hello, this is Joel." More often than not, I was so preoccupied with compiling my notes, I wouldn't get around to calling.

I've heard that women forget the pain of childbirth the moment after they've given birth. A kind of selective amnesia kicks in; it's automatic, programmed into their brains.

Apparently, this is nature's way of tricking them into even considering doing all this again. The same kind of thing must happen when two people become involved in a relationship. Let's face it: if any of us could just remember what dating was like it's my guess very few couples would ever split up. But relationships do end. And dating again, after being with one person exclusively for any length of time, requires that you learn the rules again.

Some rules don't change. For instance, any guy who is approaching forty might be forgiven for thinking that the playing field has leveled out and that it is no longer incumbent on him, as the man, to make that first, difficult telephone call. But he would be wrong.

I've heard rumors that there are actually women out there who call up guys to ask them out on a date, but, judging by my own experience, these are just rumors. Urban legends, more like it. I recognize that this may say something about me, but I've met very few guys who can claim to have been called for a first date. As for those guys who do make the claim, I prefer not to believe them.

Still, these are the nineties, so some rules have changed. The Ontario government recently funded a pamphlet entitled "Some important things for men to know about sex and dating." According to the pamphlet, any man who has ever talked a woman into having intercourse with him by "begging" has "had sex through pressure, coercion or force" and has, in effect, broken the law.

Isn't that always the way? Just when you start developing a knack for something, somebody decides to make it illegal. I doubt that I'm speaking only for myself either when I say that if you take begging away from men as a method of seduction, you may as well lock us up.

Not surprisingly, the prospect of having to date again in the current atmosphere of mistrust and misunderstanding is enough to turn Ted Kennedy into a wallflower. It's a jungle out there and now that I find myself back in the jungle, I'm looking for pointers anywhere I can find them.

Fortunately, there's no shortage of self-help manuals for people like me. These are, like I said, the nineties and not even the most natural things are expected to come naturally any more. That's why I'm not the least bit embarrassed to admit that I've been consulting *Guerilla Dating Tactics: Strategies, Tips and Secrets for Finding Romance* by psychotherapist and "certified flirting instructor" Sharyn Wolf. In her introduction, Wolf explains the overwhelming need for a book like hers: "What worked for your parents will frustrate you because it's not the old days anymore, and the old ways just don't cut it."

There are some books that make a profound difference in our lives; some books that change forever the way we experience the world. *Guerrilla Dating Tactics* isn't one of them.

Not for lack of trying, though. "When every second counts, the answer to how to meet that intriguing person rests in developing the spirit, ingenuity, and courage of the guerrilla soldier," Wolf writes.

Actually, her real message is that you will do just fine as long as you can remember to fake sincerity. Do that and you've got it made. *Guerrilla Dating Tactics*—which comes with a money back guarantee if you haven't had a date within a year of buying the book—includes advice on how to be sneaky and how to be *really* sneaky. Want to approach someone in a line in a bank? Pretend your watch is broken. Want to start a conversation with a stranger in a drugstore? Drop your change on the floor.

Wolf even has useful tips for the dating-impaired, people previously known as jerks. For example, she strongly recommends that men never look at a woman's breasts and say, "Hey, baby, your headlights are on."

In general, pickup lines are tricky, so it's always best to keep it simple. Let's face it, if you're the kind of person who's thinking about telling someone, "Sweetheart, I could drink your bath water," you're the kind of person who probably shouldn't be leaving the house at all.

Not all of Wolf's tips make sense—she never explains why you should keep a condom in your shoe. But she does operate on a simple principle: when it comes to dating, no advice is too moronic. Imagine my surprise, for example, to discover that this respected therapist and best-selling author subscribes to the same law-of-average theory as one of my old high school buddies. My buddy was convinced that if you just asked enough women to go out with you eventually one would say yes. Wolf's advice is remarkably similar. "If you don't take a chance," she says, "you don't stand a chance."

Coincidentally, Wolf also has the same philosophy of dating as another high school friend who once advised me to break out of a long dating slump by finding a crowd and standing in it. Wolf believes in crowds, singles events, sewing bees, bingo nights, personal ads, computer dating, 12-step programs, you name it. "Larry Fortensky didn't do too bad meeting Liz Taylor at the Betty Ford Clinic," she says.

If you're starting to think that the guys I hung around with in high school—guys otherwise known for best of seven belching contests—were remarkably insightful about romance, you'd be wrong. You'd be right, though, if you started to get the idea that they knew as much about dating strategies as any expert.

Take it from me: the idea that it's better to be "one for ten than zero for zero" only works in theory. Anyone who has been told by a woman he was asking out on a date, as I have, that she'll be free on July 32nd, will recognize that being zero for zero isn't so bad.

An episode of *Seinfeld* summed up the problem. Jerry is entertaining the idea of going up to a woman he's never seen before and asking her out. He believes he can do it if he can just psyche himself up beforehand. "Like those guys who walk across hot coals," he tells George. George's reply is succinct: "Sure, but those guys aren't mocked and humiliated when they get to the other side."

Obviously, I'm not a teenager any more. I know that women are probably not waiting for me to call so they can make fun of me. But there's still a part of me that doesn't want to take any chances. That's why I've dug up my old notes, searched through the table of contents and the index and have already started to work on my next opening gambit. Something subtle like: "Hello, this is Joel."

Hair Piece

Before Rogaine, government-tested shampoo, weaves and transplants, before there were Hair Clubs and Follicle Clinics, miracle cures for baldness were the exclusive domain of the neighborhood barber. Many years ago when a barber first noticed some unadorned space on the top of my head, he informed me that one day soon he'd be able to help me with "my little problem." (My bald spot was considerably smaller then.)

He whispered that he was in possession of a secret ingredient that had worked wonders with his clients in the past and he guaranteed it would work on me, too. The only problem, he said, is that I wasn't ready for it yet. Apparently, the timing had to be right. Something about the lack of viscosity in my natural oils. I didn't ask him to explain. I trusted him, the way you instinctively trust someone holding a pair of scissors next to your ear. Someone who has the additional power to make you look like a dead-ringer for Moe from the Three Stooges.

But, after a while, I started getting impatient. Each time I returned to his chair, I'd drop some subtle hint that maybe it was time for him to share his secret with me. I'd make reference to how people kept mistaking me for a monk or how cold my skull was in the winter, but he was adamant. "Soon enough," he said, "soon enough."

Carpe diem, people are always saying and for good reason. Regrettably, my barber died before he could share his secret with me. I admit that this tragic turn of events did put my own concerns about hair loss in perspective—for a while anyway. But the advent of overhead security cameras made me change my mind. There's nothing like seeing the top of your bare skull reflected in a monitor in the corner store to make you believe that death is a minor inconvenience. No wonder thieves wear ski masks and nylons and balaclavas.

Of course, what balding men need almost as much as instant hair growth is a sense of proportion. Something few of us have. I was channel surfing the other night and I paused to watch one of those ubiquitous half-hour infomercials on hair loss. In this one the host was frantically reminding his studio audience— suspiciously full of men with thinning hair, and with concerned looking spouses by their sides—that there was no need to worry any more. That's right, he said, we now have the ability to make male pattern baldness a distant memory, yesterday's news.

I surprised myself by changing the channel before the miracle cure was announced, its effectiveness guaranteed or its price dramatically reduced. It could have been anything—from a scalp massage to standing on your head for four hours every day—and, frankly, I didn't want to know. Going bald is like being involved in a bad love affair—hope is the one thing you want to avoid at all costs. Even a whisker of it can be a killer. It can lead to combovers, bad toupees, ponytails and, as I saw when I couldn't hold out any longer and finally switched back to the infomercial, the spectacle of an otherwise sensible looking man submitting his blank pate to a huckster with a spray can and uncertain aim.

I can only hope I'll never resort to spray cans, but I can't make any guarantees. I have gone through a lot of phases with my hair. In the late seventies I let it grow wild and free. I never visited a barber, never subjected it to a comb. Stylists came next, enchanting fellows with only one name. Usually Maurice. The Mousse Years followed shortly after that. Finally, there was The Great Gel Experiment of 1993.

During that period, I became so obsessed with slicking my hair back that I forgot all about my bald spot. At least, I thought, gel allows me to be in control. But, like most people who are dependent on a foreign substance, I was only fooling myself. It was the gel that was controlling me. I couldn't get enough of it. I couldn't stop putting it in my hair.

It wasn't long before I was, like Ray Milland in *The Lost Weekend,* concealing tubes in places where no one else would find them. I even kept a tube in the glove compartment of the car the way you would keep flares, in case of an emergency. But it all went sour when the woman I was seeing at the time started tracing the disturbing greasy residue on her pillow cases back to my head. Eventually, I had to take seriously her threats to contact Greenpeace and have my head declared an ecological disaster area.

That men are preoccupied with their hair will probably not come as a surprise to women. They have seen us fuss with it and fuss over it. They have tried their best and not always with success to talk us out of those toupees and combovers. All the while saying, "It doesn't matter to me. I don't care how much hair you have."

But, as with their opinions on some of our other personal endowments, we tend not to believe them. It's still open to debate who came up with the notion that baldness is a sign of virility. The obvious suspects are balding men, but it could just as easily be women who have to put up every day with the whining and insecurity of balding men.

It's the Samson myth, I suppose. I wasn't surprised, for instance, to learn that a Brazilian plastic surgeon was summoned to Tripoli recently to provide a hair transplant for Libyan president Moamar Gadhafi in order to help him maintain "the lion's mane of his youth." Clearly, even unbalanced despots, who should have more important things on their minds, stay up nights worrying about their receding hairlines.

Personally, I can't watch an episode of *Star Trek: The Next Generation* without wondering why Captain Picard is bald. I mean, here it is, the twenty-fourth century, human beings can travel at the speed of light and transport their molecules all over the galaxy, but they can't find a cure for baldness. Is this what we have to look forward to? A future in which mankind's priorities are so completely out of whack?

As for the present, I'm waiting for my new barber to reveal his secret formula. I know he has one, but, for now, he's being cagey and tight-lipped. When I started dropping hints the other day about what is, by now, my considerably bigger "little problem," he laughed and told me about a barber he used to work for in the old country who mixed hot peppers into a solution of water, oil and vinegar and then applied it to the heads of clients who were worried about losing their hair.

"Didn't that burn?" I asked.

"Sure, that was the point," my barber said. "The burning convinced his clients that something was growing. I remember he offered to give me his 'magic formula' when he retired. It's crazy what some people will believe."

"Right," I said, "and exactly what kind of hot peppers were those again? And which old country are we talking about?"

Losing the Battle of the Sexes: Or How the Toilet Seat Debate Escalated

I was in a public place recently, looking for a bathroom and thinking about something else entirely when I walked through the door marked Ladies. I'd never made that particular mistake before so I was surprised at how quickly I realized I wasn't where I was supposed to be.

Call it male intuition—that and the fact that there were no urinals in sight—but I do know I got out fast, enormously relieved no one had seen me. My hands were ice cold. My pulse was racing. I felt like a criminal. Right, I thought, this is what it means to be a man in the 1990s: you worry constantly about being misinterpreted. You overreact to everything.

Still, you think I'd be past that stage by now. Like most men, I've gotten used to women being irritated with me. I don't take it personally any more. After all, what man hasn't heard the woman in his life let out an exasperated sigh, raise her eyes and mutter the single word, "Men," as if she were calling on some higher power to explain why we do the things we do? What man hasn't been jolted out of an afternoon nap or some other pleasant reverie time and time again by the sound of the toilet seat being slammed down—the noisy gesture, invariably preceded by a small splash and a big scream, directed at us and our absent-minded behavior?

It's no coincidence that for decades women's magazines have been running banner headlines on their covers to help their readers cope with us. Some recent favorites include: "Love Lessons from Creeps, Cads and Snakes" (*Glamour*), "Love Him or Leave Him? Five Questions to Help You Decide If He's Worth It!" (*Complete Woman*), "Does He Keep Putting You Down with His Yammering Criticism?" (*Cosmopolitan*), "Your Perfect Man—Not!" (*Woman's Life*) and "Five Things You Can Change About Him" (*Mademoiselle*). The message is clear. Women view men as some sort of defective toaster on which the warranty has run out. Women can't have us fixed or get their money back, so they have to put up with burnt toast and have to learn to be grateful they haven't been electrocuted yet. It's no coincidence that the most popular male characters on television—from Archie Bunker to Homer Simpson—are dumb and getting dumber.

We've all heard the snide comments—"if they can put a man on the moon why can't they put them all there?"—and the nasty jokes. Like the one about the baby born with the characteristics of both sexes. A penis and a brain. We've all read the bumper stickers and the greeting cards. On the cover: "Birthdays are a lot like men." Inside: "The more you encounter the more you want to scream." Even Oprah, now in her kinder, gentler phase, still gets a kick, every now and then, out of pointing out how irredeemably hopeless we are.

That's why, as the twentieth century comes to a close, it's hard to blame men for thinking that women are laughing at us. I guess this shouldn't come as a surprise, but it does. My suspicion is that women have always laughed at us; the difference is that now they are doing it openly and loudly.

And why not? A strong argument could be made that we deserve the ridicule. Any gender responsible for professional wrestling, Preston Manning, Jacques Parizeau, the combover and the movie *Showgirls,* just to cite a few examples, is in no position to pretend that our personalities do not have room for improvement.

Or in a position to pretend that we really want to improve our personalities. Men are seldom happier than when we are behaving like idiots and women usually know this better than we do. Last year at my annual softball banquet one of my teammates offered a dollar to anyone at our table who would throw a dinner roll at the featured speaker, a long-winded but otherwise innocuous guy who was going on about camaraderie and the thrill of the grass. "I'll kick in an extra dollar if the roll is buttered," another teammate announced.

Now, how juvenile, how idiotic is that? Can anyone imagine a woman ever making such an offer or contemplating doing such a thing?

In my own defense, I can only say that I was aiming for his body, not his head. To his credit, the speaker, stunned for a moment as the roll bounced off his ear, leaving a smear of butter behind, just smiled and pretended nothing had happened. But then a few women at the table—some of my teammates had brought dates—glared at me. Maybe I'm overreacting again, but I saw something unexpected in their look—not just exasperation or even annoyance, both of which I expected—something like contempt.

But even if I thought it was just me, it's not. Men, as a gender, aren't as popular as we used to be. Women just don't seem to find our little habits—like leaving the toilet seat up—as endearing as they once did.

Misandry is the new word for today. The female equivalent of misogyny, it's recently started to appear in a handful of dictionaries. My first reaction when I heard that someone had finally come up with a term for man-hating was what took so long? No one can deny that the rhetoric between the sexes has become more extreme than ever; it's routine now to hear prominent feminists equating consensual sex with patriarchal oppression.

Look, I know it's not only politically incorrect but unseemly for a white North American male to be complaining about his lot in life, but male-bashing is becoming a cultural phenomenon. Besides, you know something is up when women start coming to men's defense.

In *The Princess at the Window,* just one of many books out recently which attack women for attacking men, author Donna

Laframboise argues that "feminists have rejected one brand of dogma (men are the ultimate example of everything admirable) only to adopt a new one (men are boorish swine)."

Another sure sign that the battle of the sexes is escalating is that some men have started switching sides, doing their best to become more Ms. than *Ms.* While it's true no woman who knows me or who has seen my bank account has ever accused me of being part of an oppressive ruling class, several men have. I remember speaking to a young reporter at a university newspaper once who informed me, after a brief telephone conversation, that since I was a white male it automatically followed that I was racist, homophobic and sexist. "How did you guess?" I replied.

Someone once said that "men can never be feminists, that no man has ever done better than a C+," but that hasn't discouraged them from trying and, in the process of bending over backwards, making the most idiotic comments. In the aptly titled *Refusing to Be A Man,* male feminist John Stollenberg insists that "the ethics of male sexuality are essentially rapist. The idea of the male sex is like the idea of an Aryan race."

Needless to say, these are fighting words. Until now, I've always considered myself a conscientious objector in the battle of the sexes—content to stay on the sidelines. But maybe it's time I enlisted. I already know that my battleground will be a small but symbolic one—the bathroom.

I grew up with two older sisters, I've been in and out of relationships all my life, my closest friends are females and, like the Manchurian Candidate, I've been brainwashed to think that there is no other way for the toilet seat to be except down. But now I'm starting to ask myself: Why does it have to be that way? Don't I have just as much right to have the toilet seat up? And what about those fluffy seat covers women are always buying? Don't they know how dangerous those things are? How prone they are to fall at a time when we are most vulnerable? (And why do they only seem to come in mauve or pink?) Isn't this an act of aggression? Provocation?

Of course, like all soldiers, I long for the day when there can be a lasting peace. In the meantime, though, I will remain defiant and leave the toilet seat up until things go back to the way they used to be for my gender. Until women are once again content to laugh at us behind our backs.

No More Mr. Nice Guy

This really happened: last year a man somewhere in the midwestern United States was sentenced to thirty days in jail for being a male chauvinist pig. His crime: he grunted, snorted and—it goes without saying—oinked whenever a female neighbor passed his door on her way to and from work.

But what really set this man apart from the ordinary barnyard impersonator who bothers women on the street is that he turned a whim into a serious hobby: engaging in the activity with the kind of dedication that people usually apply to becoming chess masters or professional golfers. According to the news report I heard, he'd been oinking for nine years. What's more, the noises were always directed at the same woman. So you can see that he wasn't being punished so much for his behavior, rude and distasteful though it was, as for his unflagging commitment to it.

That's why I have no doubt that once he's done serving his jail sentence, Mr. Piggy will be required to sign up for some courses in gender sensitivity training. This is the kind of thing you hear about all the time nowadays: an unenlightened football coach bans women reporters from the locker room or a lecherous university professor ogles a few coeds and, before you can say, "bad dog," they are at the mercy of psychologists and psychological tests all designed to assist them in re-evaluating their thinking and mending their ways. The idea is to combine everything social scientists have learned about brainwashing and everything veterinarians have learned about housebreaking pets and put it to a practical use.

But even though these methods sometimes work at first, they seldom have lasting results. We may prefer to believe that men who behave like hogs or hounds are a product of an environment that objectifies women, that tolerates strip clubs, lap dancing, pornography and phone sex, and we may also prefer to believe that all this can be corrected through re-education. But we'd be kidding ourselves. Like most well-intentioned plans to modify human behavior, sensitivity training has limits. A man's instinct to whistle at women is just that—an instinct.

I remember walking through shopping malls, during the Christmas rush, as a boy of eleven, with a group of friends, and purposely bumping into already distracted women in the hope that we might brush past their breasts. The thrill was minor—no one yet has been able to establish that the down-filled sleeve of a ski jacket is an erogenous zone—but it was something we felt compelled to do nevertheless. I'm embarrassed now to admit this. I don't know what I was thinking, but I guess that's the point: I wasn't thinking at all.

Take another example: the Cayapa Indians of Western Ecuador. The males in the tribe, according to anthropologists, are believed to be among the most sexually repressed in the world. They are not just shy around Cayapa women, they have an innate fear of the vagina, specifically the likelihood that their penis will be devoured by it. None of this, however, deters these sorry, messed-up guys from bragging to each other about how often they do it and with how many partners.

Thinking back, I've known my share of men who have boasted about their conquests or discussed women in sexist terms or otherwise acted like jerks. Guys, in other words, for whom an intensive weekend seminar on how not to behave like a jerk wouldn't have been such a bad idea after all.

Like the guy I used to play softball with who would summarize, in explicit detail, the plots of pornographic movies he'd just viewed. The irony was that he was courteous enough to make sure he did not tell you what happened in the end—on the off chance you were going to go out, on the strength of his word of mouth recommendation, and see *Intersextion* or *Passenger 69*. "Then she does it with two other women and this guy whose...but I won't tell you any more, I don't want to ruin it for you," he would invariably say.

I'm also reminded of a guy I worked with one summer installing air conditioners. Aside from an occasional lapse into manual labor, we spent most of our time driving a small truck around the city. It was hot and we were downtown all the time. We made a point of it, in fact. No matter where we were headed we tried to go there by way of Montreal's busiest thoroughfare, Ste. Catherine Street. Our ambition was to get stuck in traffic so we could stare at the women in their increasingly flimsy summer outfits.

But staring wasn't enough for my coworker. He also felt the need to comment on what he was seeing and his commentary took the form of honking the horn whenever an attractive woman passed by. By then I had grown out of my bumping-into-women-in-malls phase and so I wasn't happy about his unchivalrous attitude. And since he was a few years younger than me I tried to give him the benefit of my experience and—long before I'd even heard the term—conduct some gender sensitivity training of my own.

I tried to tell him that as a strategy for impressing the opposite sex, honking the horn had some drawbacks. Some serious drawbacks. For one thing, women tended not to look kindly on men in trucks anyway and frightening or insulting them could hardly be expected to improve the situation. But he went on doing it. I suppose I would have dismissed this as more his problem than mine except for one significant detail: he only honked the horn when I was driving. So I was the one behind the wheel when the inevitable dirty looks came.

The funny thing is that I now think back on that time with a certain amount of nostalgia. I didn't know it then, but it would be the last time I would be viewed as an insensitive jerk. Understand, I am not saying this to brag—just the opposite. I am a nice guy who can't help thinking, more and more, that nice is not an advantageous thing to be.

In the early 1970s, I took a psychology course in college and, for extra credit, I agreed to participate in a day-long group encounter session. After a few hours of heartfelt confessions, I was even beginning to enjoy myself. That's when the dazzling redheaded young woman sitting next to me, the woman I had been trying to impress all morning with my openness and vulnerability, turned to me and said, "I make scrambled eggs out of men like you."

This was not a threat as much as a statement of fact, a prediction. She had sized me up and decided she could wrap me around her little finger. She was right. Not much has changed since then. I am still a pushover, as transparent as Saran Wrap when it comes to women. Frankly, I am seldom attracted to anyone who can't see right through me.

Women have been bossing me around all my life—from the first time I was told to clean my room to the first time I was told how to move my feet when I was slow dancing to the first time I was told where to put my tongue...well, you get the picture.

On a night when I have a date it's not uncommon for my "To Do List" to read like this: pick up date, cook dinner, wash dishes, supply the condoms, bring date to orgasm, hold her in arms, share feelings, do not fall asleep until she does and then do not snore. Obviously, I'm exaggerating—I can't cook—but I'm not complaining. I do all this, when I have the opportunity, and I do it gladly.

Why? I suppose because I am pussy-whipped. At least that's what the more insensitive types out there might be inclined to say. Pussy-whipped is not a term that women like men to use, but men use it all the time anyway. Amongst ourselves. We say it behind each other's backs, but mostly we tease each other about it. What's worth mentioning is that we seldom push the teasing too far, perhaps because most of us acknowledge— sometimes grudgingly, sometimes happily—that it would just be a case of the pot calling the kettle black.

I should probably point out that when I talk about being "whipped" I'm not talking as much about the rules and restrictions women place on men as the impositions we place on ourselves on their behalf. Helen of Troy didn't ask the Greeks and Trojans to go to war over her and thereby change the course of history forever. No one told Van Gogh to cut off his ear. When Stendhal was writing all his novels and dedicating them to a woman who wouldn't give him the time of day, he did it without her say so. My friends who have bought houses in the suburbs, had vasectomies or opened wide to have their uvulas fried by lasers so they wouldn't snore were, for the most part, willing volunteers.

And I think the reason we fall into line is not just because we are hopeless wimps but because we recognize that we are at our best in the company of women. "I fancy myself a not untypical male in feeling that, when there is no woman in the room, the effort of making conversation is quite unnecessary: a few grunts will do," John Updike has said. "But when a woman comes into the room, or the cave or teepee, the possibilities of law, mercy, wit and affection arise. One's stutter melts, one's blood takes on a champagne simmer and sets the brain to scintillating."

None of which explains why your garden variety serial killer tends to receive a lot more love letters than I do. When a woman recently confessed to me that she thought the Unabomber was "kind of sexy," I was speechless. What could I say? Nothing, except that what we have here is just one more quirk of nature, one more cruel joke which seems to be intentionally designed to keep men who would like to treat women with respect and women who say they would like to be respected apart. I'm not blaming anyone, I'm just pointing out that it's a shame, as the character Latka once said in the sitcom *Taxi,* that "women don't like timid, weak men half as much as they should."

I know most women would say that I'm being oversensitive, probably because women are always saying that to me. "Hang in there," they will add, "nice guys are going to be the next trend. Soon there will only be nice guys and women won't have any choice."

In fact, there is some evidence to support this assertion. In a recent *Esquire* poll of 1001 men it was determined that the average man has a sexist thought only once every three days. That's still twice a week but it's a start.

Regrettably, the rest of the evidence is anecdotal and based almost entirely on my interpretation of Frank Sinatra's surprising decision a couple of years ago to alter the lyrics to his classic hit "The Lady is a Tramp" and sing "The Lady is a Champ" instead. As far as I'm concerned, the message is indisputable: even Sinatra can be sensitized. Can Arnold Schwarzenegger weeping openly in *Terminator 3* be far behind?

My real concern is whether or not these nouveau nice guys are going to be able to keep it up or if being sensitive is just a phase they're going through. My bet is it's just a phase. How do I know? Because I am the real thing, the genuine article.

I am a nice guy. Ask anyone who knows me. I am gentle, caring and trustworthy. I am loyal and considerate and respectful. I rarely leave the toilet seat up. I am a good sport and a good listener, a friend when you need one. I keep my word. I can commit—probably. I am faithful and affectionate and tender. I call the next day after sex. I buy women I am involved with little presents, I bring them flowers, I write mushy notes. I am sympathetic to PMS and menstrual cramps and I feel a certain responsibility for yeast infections. I do not forget birthdays or anniversaries or Valentine's Day. I am not afraid to cry. In fact, I cry at the drop of a hat. I am just the kind of guy women always say they would be looking for if they didn't happen to be currently involved with some heel. They even say this to me. Here's just a few of the things they've called me: a dear, a sweetheart, a pal, a buddy, a darling, a doll, a mensch, one in a million, irreplaceable. In other words, doomed.

Which is why I can't help feeling that if there was ever a candidate for insensitivity training, I'm the guy. Just wait and see: the day the course is offered, I'll be first in line at early registration. I can see the syllabus now:

The Wit and Wisdom of Andrew Dice Clay
Is Listening Overrated?

An Introduction to Belching
They Love It When You Treat Them Like Dirt:
   A Statistical Study
Leering for Beginners
Advanced Leering
Premature Ejaculation: The Bright Side

In the end, though, I know the time and the tuition would just be wasted on me. I'd come out completely and happily insensitized and then some woman would touch my hand or laugh at one of my silly jokes and I'd be scrambled eggs again. This isn't a complaint, you realize, just a prediction.

EPILOGUE

"What is a man, without his excuses?"
—Martin Amis

Homo Erectus:
Notes on the Transitional Man

While the rules for being a guy in the 1990s keep shifting, there's still one commandment of guyhood that remains unaffected by the mood and temper of our times: thou shalt not call a plumber to change a washer. No way. No how. No matter what. So far I never have.

This doesn't mean I have actually changed a washer myself. What I have done is given it lots of serious consideration, in particular the faucet that was, up until recently, leaking in the bathtub in the house in which I've lived most of my life and which my sisters and I inherited from my parents.

Mainly, what I've done is promise to repair the faucet, as one of my sisters, with whom I live, can attest. I even bought a package of assorted washers from a hardware store. I can't remember how long ago that was, I just remember when I bought them I was getting ready to graduate from high school.

In the interim, the real challenge has been keeping my sister away from *The Yellow Pages.* Whenever she gets that "I-don't-care-what-it-costs" look in her eye, I immediately spout what has so far proven to be a foolproof excuse: "How am I supposed to fix anything without the proper tools?"

My sister has been patient with me, as women generally, inexplicably are with men. She looks at me and nods a lot, pretending to understand. This is, coincidentally, the way women have looked at men from the beginning of time, from the moment the first caveman turned to the first cavewoman and said, "How am I supposed to start a fire with two sticks? Rub them together?"

Nothing has changed. Except for the bathroom faucet, which no longer leaks. A few weeks ago, I came home on Sunday night, having spent the weekend away, to receive the following domestic update from my gleeful sister:

"Al and Ray fixed it. (Al is my aunt's ninety-something beau and Ray is my other sister's husband). They used those washers you bought, remember? It took no time at all. They're going to work on the doorbell next."

Now, whenever I return home it's to discover that something else I promised to repair but never got around to is working like a charm: the doorbell was first (it needed new batteries), then the air conditioner (a new filter), then the lamp in the den (a bulb) then the smoke alarm (a battery again). One weekend, I expect to come home and find a new wing— the AL/RAY wing—added to our previously modest suburban bungalow.

I suppose all this activity should come as a relief; it should let me off the hook. Why, then, does it continue to bother me so much? The simple explanation is that when you are trying to define what it means to be a man in the final decade of the twentieth century, you'd prefer klutz not be the first word that pops into your head. Changing a washer doesn't make you a hero, but it's a start. Besides, men have always been experts at turning their most trivial achievements into profoundly significant events. How else do you explain the Super Bowl?

Changing a washer is symbolic, too—a sign that you are the man of the house, in charge, prepared for any emergency. In other words, kidding yourself.

When journalist Ian Brown travelled across North America in search of the adventurous male spirit, circa 1990, he returned with the following admission: "I never learned completely to break the back of my fear and my shame: which is to say, buck the bull, fuck the girl, ride the big wave, be a man. Instead, it's a definition I still learn every hour of the day."

That's the point, of course: there are no longer any definitions that will last us an hour or a day or a week, let alone a lifetime. Manhood is on a sliding scale these days. The rules keep changing, the ground keeps shifting. Compared to being female, being male can be pretty nonspecific. Men just don't have the same kind of biological imperatives telling us who we are and what our role is.

We don't have social imperatives any more either. Take crying, for example: we are permitted to do it in public now—we've always cried in private—but the time and place still have to be appropriate. Getting weepy during *E.T.* is appropriate; sobbing when your car stalls in traffic isn't, even if that's the time you feel most like crying.

So what can you do instead? You can curse, slap the steering wheel, get out, open the hood, stare blankly at the engine, slam the hood down, and start muttering that all you really need to get this baby going again is a monkey wrench.

Or you can face fact #1: a monkey wrench will do you as much good right now as a monkey. Fact #2: you're not Mr. Fix-It and never will be. You are Mr. Transitional.

About one million years ago when Homo Erectus decided to walk on two legs he must have sensed that things would never be the same for him again—that he could kiss his old ape habits goodbye. No more swinging from tree branch to tree branch, no more throwing his feces around. But he would have also been the first to admit that he wasn't quite ready yet for martinis, smoking jackets and *Masterpiece Theatre*.

A lot of men today find themselves in a similar position—aware they can't go back to what they were and, at the same time, unable to figure out what they are supposed to become. We are caught between a rock and a soft place: between boorish bravado and oversensitivity, Sylvester Stallone and St. Francis of Assisi. It's not a comfortable choice. It's no choice at all. Maybe, the Transitional Man is no different from anyone else nowadays: he needs role models to find his way and although it's taken me a while, I think I've found mine.

My father, who died eighteen years ago, had a difficult and a lucky life. The difficult part started when he was thirteen and contracted polio. The lucky part started some years later when he met my mother.

He was a sign painter and, unlike me, good with his hands. Like me, though, he wasn't adept at fixing things around the house. Still, he insisted on pretending he could. But he was really only in his element when he had something to paint, particularly something no one else would ever consider painting, like a favorite but faded pair of shoes—the same ones he happened to be wearing.

That's the last thing he should have been doing. Because of his polio my father fell frequently anyway and this particular pastime didn't help. His shoe would stick to the floor, he would lose his balance and go down again. When he did fall I was usually the one who picked him up. If my mother wasn't at home he'd make me promise not to say anything to her. I always kept his secret longer than he did, which wasn't very long. He told her as soon as she walked through the door. He couldn't help it. He told her everything. Aside from falling a lot, my father did a lot of other things no one, except my mother, ever expected him to. He married the woman he loved; he bought a house; he raised a family; he started a business; occasionally, he painted his shoes.

Even now, this long after his death, there are still things I can learn from him—like why it's okay to put masking tape over the rust spots on my car and how a man can be proud and dependent, capable and vulnerable all at the same time.

From my father, I learned that I can keep my emotions inside, just not for very long; I also learned, finally, that what we are is never quite as fixed as we think and neither is what we can be.

This leaves me wiser, but only a little. There are still the same eternal questions to answer. Like what do I do when the faucet starts leaking again?